COMMUNITY-BASED PSYCHOLOGICAL FIRST AID

COMMUNITY-BASED PSYCHOLOGICAL FIRST AID

A Practical Guide to Helping Individuals and Communities During Difficult Times

GERARD A. JACOBS

AMSTERDAM • BOSTON • HEIDELBERG • LONDON • NEW YORK • OXFORD
PARIS • SAN DIEGO • SAN FRANCISCO • SINGAPORE • SYDNEY • TOKYO

Butterworth-Heinemann is an imprint of Elsevier

Butterworth-Heinemann is an imprint of Elsevier
The Boulevard, Langford Lane, Kidlington, Oxford OX5 1GB, UK
50 Hampshire Street, 5th Floor, Cambridge, MA 02139, USA

Notices
Knowledge and best practice in this field are constantly changing. As new research and experience broaden our understanding, changes in research methods, professional practices, or medical treatment may become necessary.

Practitioners and researchers must always rely on their own experience and knowledge in evaluating and using any information, methods, compounds, or experiments described herein. In using such information or methods they should be mindful of their own safety and the safety of others, including parties for whom they have a professional responsibility.

To the fullest extent of the law, neither the Publisher nor the authors, contributors, or editors, assume any liability for any injury and/or damage to persons or property as a matter of products liability, negligence or otherwise, or from any use or operation of any methods, products, instructions, or ideas contained in the material herein.

British Library Cataloguing-in-Publication Data
A catalogue record for this book is available from the British Library

Library of Congress Cataloging-in-Publication Data
A catalog record for this book is available from the Library of Congress

ISBN: 978-0-12-804292-2

For information on all Butterworth-Heinemann publications
visit our website at http://www.elsevier.com/

Working together
to grow libraries in
developing countries

www.elsevier.com • www.bookaid.org

Publisher: Candice G. Janco
Acquisition Editor: Sara Scott
Editorial Project Manager: Hilary Carr
Production Project Manager: Mohanapriyan Rajendran
Designer: Matthew Limbert

Typeset by Thomson Digital

Dedication

This book is dedicated to my wife, Gera, who has been the love of my life and a tremendous support for me for 45 years in all the work I have done, and has put up with my work across the nation and around the world. It is also dedicated to my parents, John and Elizabeth Jacobs, and to my wife's parents, Charles and Charlotte Hirt. Their unconditional positive regard for people of all ethnicities, religions, and nationalities was a tremendous model for us as we developed our social skills and attitudes toward others.

TABLE OF CONTENT

ABOUT THE AUTHOR

Gerard A. (Jerry) Jacobs, PhD, is the Director of the Disaster Mental Health Institute (DMHI) and a Professor in the doctoral Clinical Psychology Training Program at The University of South Dakota. He received his PhD in clinical/community psychology from the University of South Florida in 1982. He has worked with various organizations nationally (eg, American Red Cross, American Psychological Association [APA], US Centers for Disease Control, and US Department of Defense) and internationally (eg, World Health Organization, International Federation of Red Cross and Red Crescent Organizations, Asian Disaster Preparedness Center, International Union for Psychological Science, and Japan Red Cross Society). His disaster responses have ranged from minor events to the massive loss of life and chaos of the September 11, 2001 attack on the World Trade Center, the 2001 Gujarat, India earthquake, and the 2004 Indian Ocean tsunami. He was asked to return from working on the tsunami response in Sri Lanka to set up the disaster mental health program for New Orleans after Hurricane Katrina. Dr Jacobs was an "invited exert" on the National Biodefense Science Board's (now the National Preparedness and Response Science Board) Subcommittee on Disaster Mental Health and served as a member of the National Academies of Science Institute of Medicine Committee on *Preparing for the Psychological Consequences of Terrorism* (Institute of Medicine, 2003).

Dr Jacobs is the recipient of the 2007 International Humanitarian Award from the APA Board of Directors, the 2006 Distinguished International Psychologist Award from the APA Division of International Psychology, and a 2008 award "for contributions as a humanitarian worker" from Division 48 (Society for the Study of Peace, Conflict, & Violence) and Psychologists for Social Responsibility. He has also received two APA Presidential Citation Awards. In 2008 he received an award from the International Union for Psychological Science for "outstanding worldwide critical mental health contributions to disaster relief and to training." The American Red Cross in 1995 presented him with an award for his "pioneering efforts and leadership role in the development, implementation, and nurturing of the Disaster Mental Health Services function…" Dr Jacobs was one of the first two American Red Cross National Consultants for Disaster Mental Health and held that post from 1992 to 2000. He also served on APA's Advisory Committee for the national Disaster Response Network from its inception in 1991 until 2000.

His current research program is examining the effectiveness of Community-Based Psychological First Aid for EMT's and paramedics and medical personnel. He is also studying some of the foundational aspects of traumatic stress in the Japanese cultural context in collaboration with the Muroran Institute of Technology in Hokkaido, Japan.

Gerard A. Jacobs, PhD, Director
Disaster Mental Health Institute,
University of South Dakota, Vermillion,
SD, United States

ACKNOWLEDGMENTS

So many people have supported me as I wrote this book. I first learned about community-based psychological first aid (CBPFA) from Mette Sonniks and Jean-Pierre Revel of the International Federation of Red Cross and Red Crescent Societies (IFRC). I am appreciative of all my colleagues in international humanitarian assistance, especially the IFRC International Roster for Psychosocial Support, the International Department of the American Red Cross, and those whom we served, who gave feedback, and who helped me develop this model.

My friends, students, and colleagues in the doctoral Clinical Training Program at the University of South Dakota (USD) have shown extraordinary flexibility in supporting me in work that often took me away from the university with little or no warning. Dr Randy Quevillon, our department chair, has consulted with me on the model as I developed it and provided feedback on my drafts. Dr Beth Boyd, who is currently our Director of Clinical Training, advised me on cultural matters and reviewed drafts as well. Ms Melinda Obach, an English instructor and poet at USD also provided valuable feedback on my writing. Drs Randy Quevillon, Beth Boyd, Lisa Brown, Robin Gurwitch, and Amgaa Oyungerel contributed chapters or boxes in their areas of considerable expertise. Their work is clearly credited and enriches the book.

I also want to thank my wife and children for their constant patience with me. I remember one major aviation disaster that occurred on my twin daughters' 12th birthday. The news was broadcasted during their birthday party. I looked at them and one of them said, "Its okay, Dad. Go. We understand that right now they need you more than we do." The Red Cross called and I left for the crash site.

Finally, my thanks to you, those reading this book, who have an interest in supporting your family, friends, and neighbors during difficult times. I hope that this book will serve you well.

WHAT IS COMMUNITY-BASED PSYCHOLOGICAL FIRST AID?

Introduction

The experience of stress is an inescapable part of the human condition. Daily life is filled with decisions, choices, problems, and a variety of other challenges with varying degrees of difficulty. Generally, we deal with these challenges without even considering the stress involved. We do what we need to do to make it through the day. The great majority of these events probably do not even register in our awareness as stressful. We either fit these events into our personal view of the world (assimilation) or alter our view of the world to fit the events (accommodation).

From time to time, however, everyone experiences events that require more than the average psychological energy. For example, if you are a parent, perhaps your child will misbehave or act out from time-to-time more than usual. In those moments, you need to refocus your energy, helping the child to both stop the inappropriate behavior and learn more appropriate ways to get what he or she wants. People occasionally are involved in an automobile accident. Even if no one is hurt in the accident, there will be a certain amount of extra psychological energy needed to deal with the hassles of paperwork, having the damage to the car repaired, dealing with an insurance claim, or perhaps finding alternate transportation for a while. If someone is hurt in the accident, the event requires even more mental energy. The energy required to cope with the event escalates further if someone files a lawsuit (that is true even for the person filing the lawsuit).

psychological/ mental energy

Sometimes the world has unpleasant surprises in the form of disasters, whether natural (eg, floods, storms, earthquakes),

Community-Based Psychological First Aid. http://dx.doi.org/10.1016/B978-0-12-804292-2.00001-6

technological (eg, hazardous materials spills, aviation disasters), or intentional (eg, terrorist attacks or criminal acts such as assault or robbery). How many of us who are old enough remember where we were when we learned of the attacks of September 11, 2001? Do you remember the images, the emotions, the confusion? Unless you are too young, you probably remember the impact that those attacks had on many Americans. In addition, however, in the months that followed, wherever I traveled in Europe and Asia, citizens of many nations wanted to express to me their sorrow about the attacks, and spoke of the tremendous emotional and psychological impact the attacks had on them, even though they were not Americans. The world expended a great amount of psychological energy that day and in the days that followed.

Think about how you, as an individual, respond to any of these more stressful events. As events increase in stress, most people are likely to turn to family members and friends to talk about the experiences, may be even discuss ways to cope with the events. Some events may be sufficiently stressful that the usual support of family and friends proves to be insufficient, and individuals may turn to physicians or spiritual leaders for additional guidance and/or support. Usually, only when the events are particularly stressful do people turn to mental health professionals to get some professional support in working through more difficult life events and decisions. (Do note, however, that mental health professionals can also be useful in less stressful moments in life.)

Throughout much of the world, when people experience physical injuries they typically try first to manage the injury themselves. They may use techniques learned through traditions in their cultures, or those that were taught to them by their parents, or those that they learned in school. If the injury is bad enough, they may seek help from others. These others may include individuals with some formal training in first aid, or, in more serious events and in countries where such expertise is available, emergency medical technicians, paramedics, or medical professionals at a clinic or hospital. In some countries, getting and staying trained in first aid is considered a civic obligation. Some countries even require adults to have a first aid certificate in order to get or renew a driver's license.

Every culture and community also has its own ways of coping with stressful events and managing psychological reactions to difficult moments in life. In the past decade, there has been a growing movement in the world to develop a set of skills for coping with stressful events that would work similarly to the way that first aid is used to cope with physical injury. This strategy has been known by a number of names, but is most commonly referred to as psychological first aid (PFA). Community-based PFA (CBPFA), the specific model of PFA that I will describe in this book, began with programs in Scandinavia, particularly in Denmark, and has been significantly adapted based on my more than 30 years as a clinical/community/disaster psychologist working in more than 30 countries around the world.

Essentially, CBPFA provides individuals with skills they can use in coping with the stress in their own lives, as well as stress in the lives of their family, friends, neighbors, classmates, or coworkers. At the core, these skills include a knowledge of stress and extreme or overwhelming (traumatic) stress, effective "active listening" skills, and knowledge about how to help someone get other forms of psychological support if CBPFA proves inadequate. The CBPFA model of PFA builds on the strengths of the community in which the individual lives and provides a more systematic understanding of how to cope with difficult moments and periods in life.

Providing CBPFA begins with caring about the welfare of the person experiencing stress. Knowledge of stress and traumatic stress helps you to know whether the person is experiencing an ordinary reaction to an extraordinary event in life, or if the person may be experiencing a more severe (pathological) reaction (this is fairly rare). If the person is having an ordinary stress reaction, PFA will help you know how to provide effective psychological support through truly effective listening, and possibly through the provision of practical assistance such as problem-solving or helping the person to meet practical needs such as food or shelter (sometimes referred to as "instrumental assistance"). If the person is having a response that is beyond the scope of PFA, this book will also help you understand how to help the individual get the psychological support that he/she needs to return the psychologically healthiest life possible.

TRY THIS

To begin, it may be useful to think about the past year. What difficult times occurred in your own life, in the lives of your family, friends, colleagues? Can you identify times when you wish you could have done more to support those you care about? This book will provide you with the tools to provide the best support you can in the future.

It Is Not Always Obvious

While I was writing this book, a friend approached me and asked me to specifically mention in this book that it is not always obvious when someone is experiencing a nearly overwhelming stress. They had recently received word of a cancer diagnosis, a significant stressor that many of us will need to cope with at some point in life. Trying to go about their normal activities in their job, they talked about a sense of disconnect, with people talking about issues in the workplace that suddenly seemed unimportant to the newly diagnosed person. While others talked about this report or that event, my friend said, they were thinking about how to ensure that their children would be cared for, the financial implications, and the imminent possibility of death. This lead them to think about how many people must be struggling with personal crises that no one around them knows about. How nice it would be, they said, if we all knew that there were people around us who were ready to reach out and listen and support us through such difficult times.

Some Cautionary Notes

CBPFA does not involve psychotherapy. Learning CBPFA does not mean that you are becoming a mental health professional. That would require an undergraduate university degree, followed by years of graduate study in one of the mental health fields. Rather, CBPFA will improve your skills in taking care of yourself and in providing basic psychological support for family, friends, neighbors, and colleagues, especially at difficult moments in life.

It is important to understand the limitations of CBPFA. It can be a very useful technique for people working through and recovering from difficult episodes in their lives or simply dealing with the daily hassles of life. But it is not intended to cure psychological disorders. Please be sure to read each of these chapters so that you will be clear on what CBPFA can and cannot do, and how to help those who need something more than CBPFA.

It is also important to recognize that a book such as this can only provide enough information to get you started. As you develop your skills, it may be useful for you to seek out additional training or educational materials to enhance your knowledge and skills.

PFA in a Community Context

This book describes a model of PFA that may be useful as a starting point. It certainly will not teach you everything you could learn about this topic. But it is intended to cover the basic information needed to begin providing CBPFA.

Within the United States there are many thousands of different communities, with different religious, ethnic, socioeconomic, and cultural differences that make each one of them unique. Many of these communities also have unique ways of coping with stress. This book's PFA model, CBPFA will be most effective if you adapt it to your own life and the life of your community. But just as there are some universal procedures in physical first aid, there are also some clear facts about how people respond to stress, and what techniques are likely to be useful in responding to those events.

Again, I encourage you to read this entire book before beginning to provide CBPFA. A number of these chapters present information that may affect the way you provide CBPFA. Among other topics, these chapters include some critical issues such as the limitations of CBPFA, how to avoid harming those whom you want to help, when to refer someone to a mental health professional, and guidelines to follow in order to be an ethical helper. Considerations in providing CBPFA to older adults, to those with disabilities, to those living in marginalized cultures, and to those in rural communities will also be discussed.

ON BEING A HELPER
AND PROVIDING CBPFA

In many cultures around the world, members of communities presume that if something difficult happens to them or to their families, their neighbors and other members of their community will come to their assistance. In the United States, this is seen in events such as barn-raisings within Amish and Mennonite communities, fund-raisers to help cover medical expenses of seriously ill or injured children and adults, church groups preparing meals for families who have experienced a death, farmers coming together to help an ailing neighbor harvest crops, or hundreds and even thousands of volunteers from outside the area helping build sandbag dikes to prevent flooding due to rising rivers.

Similarly within families there is often an expectation

Community effort to fill sandbags to prevent flooding of neighbors' homes.

that if one member has a difficult experience, other members of the family will be there for them to provide support. Not all families meet these expectations, however, and all families probably fall short of this goal some of the time. It is also true that the support available within even the ideal family may not be adequate to meet some needs of family members for psychological support, particularly after traumatic events or events that directly affect multiple members of the family.

Many people are comfortable participating in such support activities if they can do so as part of a group, but feel shy, embarrassed, or uncomfortable in reaching out alone to support those in need. Some people are perhaps *too* comfortable reaching out and can become intrusive, leading to discomfort in those whom they intend to support. Since CBPFA will generally be provided on a more individual basis, this chapter addresses how to be comfortable and appropriate when you are serving as a helper.

The Art of Helping

Mette Sonniks served for a number of years as the Director of the International Federation of Red Cross and Red Crescent Societies' Reference Centre for Psychosocial Support in Copenhagen, Denmark. The Reference Centre is basically the Federation's world center for psychosocial support. She was fond of quoting Soren Kirkegaard, a Danish existentialist philosopher. Mette felt that one particular quotation embodied "the secret art of helping" and precisely described the attitude which will be most useful to you as a helper in giving someone who needs psychological support the assurance that you offer him or her true empathy and support:

> " *If one is truly to succeed in leading a person to a specific place, one must first and foremost take care to find him where he is and begin there." (Kierkegaard, 1948/1998, p. 48).*

Essentially, Kierkegaard maintained that helpers must begin by listening to the person whom they intend to help, and, through that listening assess the needs of the individual at that moment in time as well as the resources with which the individual has to work. If we truly want to help, it is not effective to simply provide the same exact support to every person or in every circumstance. Each specific individual at any given moment in life is likely to need a unique blend of support strategies. If many individuals have been affected by an event, each one is likely to be at a different point in reacting to the event and is likely to be further along in recovery than some people, and not as far along as others. By understanding each individual's or family's needs at the beginning, it is possible to select the specific psychological support tools which may be most useful at that specific point in time for the people whom you want to support. As will be discussed later in this book, this is often accomplished through effective listening.

Carl Rogers, a famous American psychologist, addressed this issue in a slightly different way. Rogers was a highly respected theorist who spent a great deal of his career studying the importance of the relationship between someone in need of psychological support and someone trying to provide that needed support. To paraphrase his writings, there are three things required in order to truly provide psychological support: (1) Two or more people need to be present and one needs to have less need for psychological support than the other(s) at that moment in time. (2) The person with less need for psychological support needs to genuinely care about the other person whose need for psychological support is greater. (3) The person(s) with greater need of psychological support must be aware that the other person genuinely cares. If we can accomplish these three steps, according to Rogers, psychological support occurs. Of course, if that were all we needed to consider, this book could end here, and Rogers would not have written his many books about how to best accomplish these three seemingly simple steps.

[handwritten margin note: Rogers says 3 things are needed to provide psychological support]

Characteristics of Effective Helpers

A helper needs to concentrate on serving the needs of the person whom the helper seeks to support. It is important that the helper not be invested in accomplishing some personal goal; the goal of the helper needs to be to support. A domineering or controlling attitude or personality will not provide effective psychological support.

The danger of describing characteristics that can contribute to being an effective helper is that it is possible to quickly build an unattainable goal of becoming some nearly perfect angel of mercy, a Florence Nightingale figure with divine selfless qualities. Although it might be nice, and we may all aspire to steadily become better people, it is extremely important to remember Rogers' three criteria for providing psychological support. We do not need to be perfect. We can provide support if, at that point in time, we have less need for psychological support than the person(s) whom we hope to serve, and if we care about the other person(s). Having said that, however, it is still useful to think about what skills or characteristics can help us to be more effective helpers.

Perhaps the most basic quality for a PFA helper is "approachability." If people find someone a little frightening because she/he often gives an angry scowl or a harsh word when someone approaches him/her, they are less likely to approach that person when they need psychological support. People in need are also less likely to welcome such a person if the person approaches them.

So, it is useful to consider: What characteristics in you affect how comfortable someone is likely to be in approaching you? Approachability is often established well before you come to the point of providing psychological support. Some of the factors that increase approachability have to do with one's reputation in the family or community. Perhaps most critical among these is being "trustworthy." If people know that they can trust you to maintain their privacy they are far more likely to accept you or even seek you out as a helper.

CASE EXAMPLE

One high school teacher whom I respect a great deal talked to me about how amazed they were to learn about some of the struggles that their students face, both in life outside of the school setting, and in the interpersonal pressures within the school. But the students do not talk about those things until a real sense of trust has developed between the student and teacher through the usual daily routine of school life. They have talked about how they try to overcome their initial reactions when they see students with messy clothes and hair, or have students turn in assignments late or fail exams. Teachers who treat students with respect, even when the teacher needs to enforce classroom discipline, even if the students are turning in assignments late, who offer to work with students at school before and after the usual school day, become approachable. Then the students can venture to take the risk and reach out for support.

I once heard an elementary school principal addressing a teacher's meeting. I was deeply moved by his words, "You don't know what a child has gone through just to make it to your classroom." One documentary first showed a group of children in the classroom, all looking like typical school children. Then the scene switched to one of those children getting ready for school earlier that morning. The child woke up in a car with their mother and siblings. The child walked to a nearby gas station and used the restroom to wash up for the day as best they could. Then the child returned to the car to put on school clothes and walked to school and blended into the classroom of children.

A close friend of mine is a highly intelligent, well-educated, socially skilled individual working in a support capacity in a professional firm and raising a family. They shared with me that they had grown up in an extremely dangerous part of a major city. As a young child and into the teen years, street gangs were a part of life, and if you were not a gang member, you were routinely threatened, physically assaulted, robbed, and sometimes sexually assaulted. Because of the location of the family's home and the school, each day they had to cross the borders of three different street-gang territories in order to get to school. And after school they had to do it again just to get home. Each day included terror. The fight for survival was an immediate and real daily battle. Did the teachers in that school understand what the daily lives of some of their students were like?

These points do not relate just to teachers, however. How many of those around us are struggling to portray an organized life, even while they battle enormous life stressors? It is very important to have approachable people ready to provide psychological support. Approachability is certainly dependent to some extent on how you behave in the moment. But even more so it is the way you live your life and the respect you give to people on a daily basis.

Other characteristics of an effective helper are more likely to be exhibited in the process of providing CBPFA. If you have already looked over the Table of Contents for this book, you may have seen that Chapter 6 deals with "active listening." Having good listening skills is an extremely useful quality for helpers. Again, there are related qualities that contribute to being a good listener. A "caring attitude" can be immediately apparent to people. Other characteristics can be more easily appreciated as people begin to interact, including "kindness," "patience" (eg, as people take time struggling to find words to express their feelings, or with constant interruptions in the discussion for family duties), "empathy" (ie, communicating the genuine caring you feel for the person whom you are trying to support), and being "nonjudgmental" as things are discussed.

Finally, some characteristics such as "commitment" may only become apparent with the development of the relationship over time. Are you available to provide support when needed? Do you give the person whom you are supporting your undivided attention as they tell you their story or their concerns? Of course, there are limits to how much you can make yourself available. You need to maintain your own personal life, maintain self-care, and fulfill your commitments to your family, school or work, and other areas of your life in addition to your commitment to providing psychological support.

Accepting Yourself in the Role of a Helper

Raising negative issues early in a discussion is often discouraged in communication theory. In other words, it can be unprofitable to talk about what might be characteristics that would make you a less-effective listener. But in examining your role as a helper, it seems important to address some possible personal concerns, because these issues can sometimes prevent a prospective helper from following through and learning how to provide CBPFA.

As mentioned earlier in this chapter, some individuals may be comfortable helping others as a member of the group, but may feel personally embarrassed or concerned about helping in a one-to-one situation. Feelings that people have often expressed about this experience include: (1) being afraid that the person to whom you are offering support will be rude and there will be rejection when you reach out; (2) being concerned that the needs of the individual(s) receiving the support may be greater than your skills can effectively serve, and therefore you may feel weak or unqualified; (3) fear of being intrusive; (4) fear that embarrassing details about those being supported may be shared in the CBPFA; or even (5) fear of personal danger in providing CBPFA in people's homes. Let us explore each of those concerns.

Rudeness and Rejection

Here is the honest truth. If you offer many individuals and families CBPFA, you are likely to experience some rejection. It is possible that sometimes rejection will be done in a rude fashion, although I have very rarely experienced rudeness in reaching out to others in a caring way. Some people will not appreciate your efforts and may even see your offers as intrusive and inappropriate. That is real, and to use an old expression, "It comes with the territory." Try not to take it personally. Most often such rudeness is likely to be an attempt by the individual or the family to maintain control of their own environment—a common and often important coping strategy, especially in times of great stress. It can also result because of people's uncertainty and fear in the situation.

Other times, people might reject your offer simply because they are not ready to deal with their experiences in this way. If you care about the individuals and families whom you are trying to serve, rejection by some will not prevent you from persevering and reaching out to others. And remember, rude rejections are extremely likely to be the exception, not the rule. I have done this type of work for more than 30 years in communities across the nation and around the world, and I have seen very few instances of such rudeness.

Concern That Your Own Skills as a Helper May Not Be Adequate

If you provide CBPFA to many people, you will most likely encounter some people whose needs will be greater than your skills, or at least people whose needs are different from the skills that you bring to the situation. For what it is worth, this is also true for licensed mental health professionals. It is important for a CBPFA helper (or a mental health professional) to quickly recognize when this situation occurs. When this happens, a referral needs to be made to a helper or professional whose skills better fit the needs of the individual or family. There is no need to be concerned or embarrassed about making referrals to others. This is an everyday part of life even for mental health professionals who have very advanced training.

Fear of Being Intrusive

Certainly this is a valid concern. It is important not to force CBPFA on anyone. But if you offer support in a polite, caring, and supportive manner to someone in need, it will be only a minimal intrusion if they reject your offer and you respectfully leave. On the other hand, if they accept the support you offer, your assistance may be a powerful tool in their healing process. The potential benefits in this case far outweigh the risk.

Fear of Learning Embarrassing Details

This is also a valid concern in CBPFA. It is quite possible that at times you may find that some of the information shared with you is embarrassing. The counter to this is to remember that the needs of the person you are serving are more important at that moment than your own needs. If your embarrassment serves no useful purpose, set it aside and focus on how you can best provide support.

Fear of Personal Danger

This is a concern that should be taken very seriously. In my experience, helpers do not think about this issue often enough, and take unnecessary and unwise risks. If you are trying to provide support to people whom you do not know, consider working in teams of two. It is always a good idea for someone you trust to know where you will be while providing PFA, and when you expect to return. If you have a cell phone and there is cell service, you can always update your plans.

Even if you are providing support to family, friends, or coworkers, it is important to consider that individuals who are experiencing traumatic stress may act quite differently from their ordinary daily behavior. Therefore, it is useful to consider safety issues even when dealing with people you know.

With regard to this concern, it is important to trust your own instincts. If you feel a situation is unsafe, do not proceed. If you are going to make a mistake regarding safety, make the error on the side of keeping yourself safe. Proceeding under the umbrella of misplaced courage will serve no purpose if you wind up needing instead of providing psychological support.

TRY THIS

A simple way to begin to explore the role of helper is to set aside the idea of psychological support at first. Look for opportunities to just be helpful. If someone is preparing a meal or doing dishes, offer to help. If you see a neighbor shoveling snow, offer to join them. If someone in your family is cleaning a room or performing some other household task, offer to do it together. Chores can often be fun if done together.

CASE EXAMPLE

In my undergraduate course on CBPFA (and in several of my other courses) I have had an assignment that students need to perform every 2 weeks during the course. They are required to "spend at least 1 hour performing some altruistic act. An altruistic act is an act done to benefit someone else, without any expectation of benefit or recompense for yourself. This may include such things as helping someone move, visiting an elderly resident of the nursing home, helping an older resident shovel snow, serving at a local meal program serving the poor, or a host of other activities, as long as they are truly altruistic. Note that these things that you try need to be something new, not a routine or ongoing obligation you already have, such as babysitting for a family member. For each of these altruistic acts write a journal about your feelings and reactions to it. No more than one page typewritten in length. Every year students grumble about the assignment, asking how this is related to psychology. And every year on their anonymous course evaluations, many of the students say that the altruistic acts were a very important learning experience for them. Many students have told me that they continue the habit of reaching out to someone even after the course has finished. The point of the assignment, of course, is to help the students learn how to be a helper.

How to Begin

Finally, if you are uncomfortable with the thought of being a helper, here are some suggestions for getting started. (1) Start with providing support within your family, or within a circle of friends with whom you feel comfortable. It may even be helpful to tell them that you are trying to learn how to be more supportive and ask for their patience as you practice. I have very often been told that friends and family tend to be very supportive of such efforts, and may even want to learn the techniques themselves. (2) Then try reaching outside that circle of family and friends. Nothing breeds confidence like success. If you can work through a few false starts or rejections, you may find yourself becoming more and more comfortable in the role of a helper. (3) Think about working with a partner as a team. You can draw strength and support from one another, and learn from one another as well.

Reference

Kierkegaard, S. (1998). *The Point of View*. Hong H.V. & Hong E.H. (Trans.). Princeton: Princeton University Press, pp. 48.

3

INDIVIDUAL DIFFERENCES IN RESPONSES TO STRESS

Every reader of this book could probably develop a long list of events and situations that can be very stressful in life. Surprisingly, though, every life experience on such a list can lead to a wide variety of reactions by different people experiencing them, or even by the same person experiencing similar events on different occasions. There is very clear evidence of the principle of individual differences in response to stress. Two examples may serve to illustrate these differences.

Years ago, a psychologist was asked to consult with a company that included a control room in which three employees guided trains from various points of origin to various destinations, hopefully avoiding other trains and delays in the process. Two of these employees had suffered recent heart attacks. The company leaders knew that stress was one component in the development of heart disease. Therefore they asked the psychologist to assess the work stress involved in those positions, with an eye toward protecting employees in those positions from further heart disease. Immediately upon entering the control room it was obvious to the psychologist that the stress involved in the job was perceived differently by the three employees on duty at the time. All were very good at their job, and kept the trains moving quickly and safely. But two of them were obviously stressed, looking very worried and nervously uttering exclamations and occasional expletives as they rapidly moved from control to control guiding the trains assigned to them. The third employee appeared to be having the time of his life, jumping from control to control and humming and talking to himself in a delighted tone of voice about each step he needed to

Community-Based Psychological First Aid. http://dx.doi.org/10.1016/B978-0-12-804292-2.00003-X

execute to keep the trains moving quickly and safely. He seemed to think of this as a giant model railroad or an exciting video game. Guess which of the employees was the one that had *not* suffered a heart attack! They all had the same workload, the same tasks, roughly the same experience and level of skill. Yet for two of them this was a grueling and even painful task, and for the third it was fun. Objectively an observer would probably define the task as stressful. But individuals can see things differently.

Much of my disaster experience has involved transportation incidents involving the deaths of large numbers of people. Most people would agree that the process of recovering the remains of those who have died in such situations is very stressful. In every instance I have experienced, the recovery workers treated the human remains with intense respect, and wanted the families of those who died to know that their loved ones were treated with great care in the recovery process. Since 1994, the workers recovering human remains have generally worn biohazard suits to protect them from possible diseases carried by those who died. These suits are very uncomfortable, and the work is often physically demanding. However, the stress levels of the recovery teams differ from incident to incident.

I have not done the scientific research to prove it, but I would maintain that there is a tremendously greater amount of stress for recovery teams whose members do not usually work with human remains, compared to teams for whom body recovery is a common part of their job. Furthermore, I have met a small number of workers who do this work professionally and who report that they experience no stress in performing their jobs. They have told me that, in their worldview, all people die eventually, and for the people who died in that particular incident this was their day. These workers said that they simply accept the fact that people die as an ordinary part of life. Some of my colleagues have questioned whether these workers were being truthful and whether such an attitude is possible. But I am convinced that even events that the great majority of people see as overwhelmingly stressful are seen by other people as routine and unremarkable experiences.

A Model of Individual Reactions to Stress

So what are some of the factors that contribute to whether an event is experienced as stressful? Charles D. Spielberger, who was one of the world's leading theorists on human responses to psychological stress, proposed a model in 1966 that attempted to explain individual differences in response to stressful events. Although more complex models have since been proposed by various theorists, Spielberger's model remains an effective approach

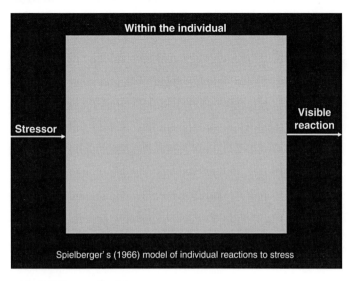

Within the individual

Stressor

Visible reaction

Spielberger's (1966) model of individual reactions to stress

Figure 3.1. Spielberger Model a.

for understanding some of the factors involved in individual differences in responses to events (Fig. 3.1).

This model simplifies the portrayal of individual reactions to stress in a number of ways in order to make it easier to understand some of the factors that affect these complex processes. First, it represents all stressors as coming from outside the individual. Of course we generate some stressors within ourselves through our self-talk. Everyone talks to themselves. We often put pressure on ourselves to meet expectations that we have either created for ourselves or accepted from others. Many people rethink how they could have acted in a situation that just occurred (eg, "Did I say the right thing in talking with that person? Could I have done better? Did I end too quickly or not quickly enough?").

Responses to stressors are represented in this model as visible behavior. Of course there are also responses to stress that are internal (eg, gastrointestinal upset such as nausea, emotions that are not revealed to the outsider, increased heart rate and blood pressure, headache).

Spielberger suggested that the very first step in processing a stressful event is cognitive appraisal. This is a fancy way of saying that each person decides almost instantly whether they need to be concerned about some event about which they become aware. This may happen thousands of times each waking hour. The huge majority of things that we sense (ie, hear, taste, touch, see, smell) we quickly dismiss as unimportant or not worthy of our attention and energy. For example, every spot where our clothing is touching

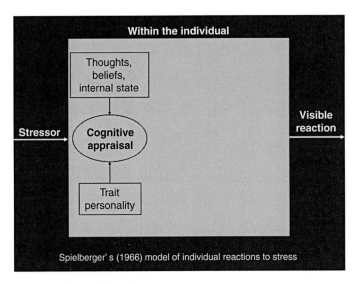

Figure 3.2. Spielberger Model b.

us triggers touch sensors in the skin, but for the most part, the brain ignores those signals. But if the pattern of touch signals sent to the brain suggests that something is moving between our skin and our clothes (such as an insect), the brain will quickly focus our attention on that sensation (Fig. 3.2).

Various factors may affect our cognitive appraisal. Trait personality, one of those factors, refers to the way we generally feel and behave from day to day across time. It is partially determined by our inherited genetics, and partially by the sum of all the things we have learned throughout our lives. Other factors include our thoughts, beliefs, and internal state. Most people have experienced watching a scary movie and telling themselves, "This is not real. Do not be afraid." This is an example of how we can help control our reactions through our thoughts. But thoughts can also lead us to become more stressed in response to a stimulus. We may hear a sound in our house late at night, and think to ourselves, "There have been burglaries in the neighborhood." Such thoughts can heighten our awareness of other sounds, make it difficult to fall back to sleep, or can even result in nightmares. Our beliefs can also affect our cognitive appraisal. If someone is rude to us, and we believe that everyone "should" treat us nicely, we are likely to experience more stress than if we believe that some people may be rude simply because they had a bad day. The final factor that directly affects our cognitive appraisal is how we feel both physically and psychologically at the time. Our physical state is important. If we are not well-rested, are hungry, or are in pain, things seem more stressful. If our psychological state is anxious,

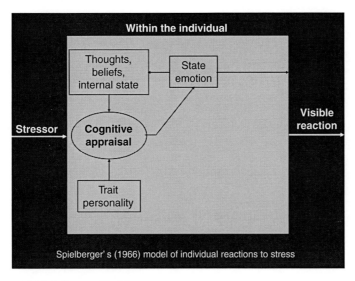

Figure 3.3. Spielberger Model c.

or angry, or sad, or otherwise negative, we are more likely to judge experiences as more stressful (Fig. 3.3).

Whether we find something stressful or not, our appraisal adjusts our emotional state (how we feel at that moment), and that emotional state is part of our internal state. And the internal state, as described previously, affects the cognitive appraisal, which affects our emotional state, which affects our internal state, and so on. This can result in a spiraling increase in stress.

spiral

If we should decide that something has the potential to be a problem for us, this leads to a series of nearly simultaneous and constantly adjusting reactions. There is an immediate emotional response, even if that response is small. If we are in a fairly comfortable state when this process begins, the immediate response is likely to be fairly calm, often consisting of an "orienting response," in which we simply begin to pay more attention to the event to monitor it more carefully.

If, on the other hand, we are already feeling fairly stressed, even the immediate emotional response is likely to be somewhat exaggerated. If we are already angry, we are likely to become more angry. If we are anxious, we become more anxious, and so on. We have similar parallel reactions in our cognitive, behavioral, and physical systems. These reactions are all interrelated. When the system works well, it serves to help us to orient to and further evaluate genuine stressors that we are experiencing. If, however, we are already significantly stressed when we sense a new event, the preexisting stressful condition makes it more likely that we will decide the new event is threatening in some way (Fig. 3.4).

If we are already feeling stressed or angry this just increases

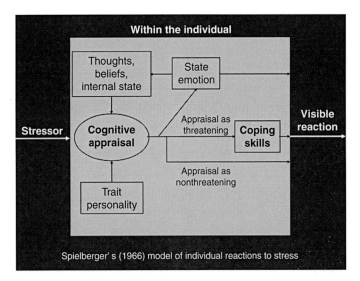

Figure 3.4. Spielberger Model d.

When the individual's initial judgment is that the new stressor poses some level of threat or need for a response, the individual reviews his/her virtual "bag of coping skills" to determine what tools the individual has to cope with the new stressor. These coping skills may include a wide variety of resources, including specific coping skills, knowledge about the stressor through education or experience, or previous successes in dealing with similar stressors (Fig. 3.5).

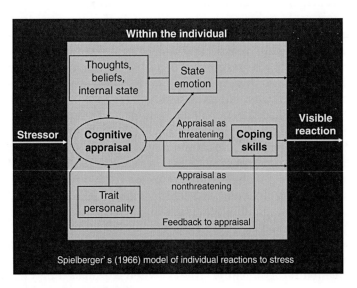

Figure 3.5. Spielberger Model e.

If we find that our bag of coping skills gives us effective tools to respond to the event, we take comfort in that. This in turn provides feedback to our cognitive appraisal, and we are more likely to interpret the event as less threatening. On the other hand, if we check our bag of coping skills and do not find any relevant tools to deal with the event, this also provides feedback to our cognitive appraisal. In essence, the feedback is something like, "Okay, now it is really time to worry." This can lead to a spiraling increase in stress reactions.

understanding the need for coping skills

Two Examples to Illustrate the Model

A woman in labor with her second child suddenly experienced a dramatic increase in labor pains. This produced an immediate orienting response, as she increased her attention to the source of the pain, and wondered immediately whether something may have gone wrong with the baby. This fear led to an immediate increase in muscle tension. This increase in muscle tension, in turn, directly increased the pain. The woman was able to focus through the pain, and checked her coping skills to determine what she could do to cope with the pain.

Among her coping skills was knowledge from her childbirth preparation classes, and this provided the realization that the increase in pain probably meant that the labor had entered the "transition" phase. She knew that this phase is usually fairly short and usually comes near the end of labor. She also remembered, with the help of her childbirth coach (another coping resource), that there are specific breathing and concentration techniques reserved for the transition phase, and she began using those techniques. She also recalled memories from the birth of her first child, and comforted herself with the knowledge that she had dealt with this phase successfully before.

When we dig into our bag of coping skills and find knowledge about the stressor, relevant previous experience, or specific skills to cope with the stressor, this provides comforting feedback to our own cognitive appraisal process and the threat assessment is reduced to some extent. In the case of the woman moving into the transition phase of labor, the knowledge, skills, and memories of her previous successful labor reduced the threat of the suddenly increased pain, and those coping resources reduced the tension somewhat, and thus actually reduced the physical pain.

The effect of having coping skills.

In contrast, if a woman is in the same situation, but is in labor for the first time, has not had childbirth preparation classes, does not know about the transition stage of labor, does not have a childbirth coach, and has only experienced pain of this intensity in a previous miscarriage, her feedback to her cognitive appraisal process may lead to even greater fear and pain. The two women experience similar situations, but with very different reactions.

So let us consider a different example. I apologize for the following example if you have a fear of snakes. If you do, you may want to skip to the **Each Person's Response is Unique** heading.

Imagine that a professor is teaching a seminar to a group of four students. At the beginning of one class, the professor walks in with a very large boa constrictor snake, which he proceeds to place on the floor in the middle of the students who are seated in a circle. All of the students experience the same stimulus. It is the same snake for each student. It is the same distance away from each student. Yet the reactions of the students may vary dramatically, one student leaping to his feet and running out of the room; one jumping atop a nearby table; one rather calmly drawing his chair further away from the snake; and one approaching the snake and stroking it gently. So there is one situation, but many reactions. What could account for these differences? Again, let us turn to Spielberger's model.

For the student who leapt up and ran out of the room, we might guess that the student's cognitive appraisal was that the snake posed a serious physical threat. Perhaps the student's trait personality (ie, the way a person generally feels) includes trait anxiety levels well above average. It's also possible that the student's physical state, which affects cognitive appraisal, was not at its best—maybe from lack of sleep from partying or from cramming for a test. This student's immediate response may also represent an instinctual response to the perceived threat.

Similarly, the student who jumped up on a table probably perceived the snake as a threat, possibly for reasons similar to the first student. Her response may differ from the first student's because when she reached into her bag of coping skills she discovered that when she had been threatened by an animal in the past, she was able to escape by climbing above the threat. (If this were a genuine threat in the real world, it would be an unfortunate error to climb on the table, because boa constrictors in the wild climb trees to get their dinner—a *little* knowledge can genuinely be a dangerous thing.)

The student who pushed back a little from the snake may have decided the snake was not an immediate threat, but was worth continuing attention. When he reached into his bag of coping skills he found knowledge about boas from watching *Animal Planet* or *National Geographic Channel*. So he knew, or thought he knew, that boa constrictors: (1) do not move very quickly; (2) do not strike their prey; (3) eat infrequently; and (4) would probably not be able to eat an adult human. Furthermore, his belief system told him that a professor is unlikely to do something that would endanger students in a class.

Finally, the student who approached the snake probably did not see the snake as a threat. She may have an adventurous trait personality or a belief in trying new things. Having decided the snake was not an immediate threat, she may have discovered in her coping skills a thorough knowledge of boa constrictors from having one as a pet, or having read about them.

Each Person's Response is Unique

In the face of identical situations, Spielberger's model can explain a wide variety of individual reactions to stressful events. When you reach out to provide psychological support, realize that everyone who experienced an event is likely to have a different response to the event. You may find that some individuals are having strong reactions, whereas others are having very little reaction. Both of these responses can be ordinary responses to extraordinary events.

TRY THIS

Think back over the past year (or whatever time frame is useful for you). Choose a time when you felt afraid. Do you remember whether there was anyone in the situation who reacted differently? If you do not remember being afraid, you can substitute anger or sadness. You can also flip the roles if you remember a time when someone else reacted emotionally and you felt calm. Can you guess at an explanation for why you had different reactions?

How Someone Can be Helped to Reduce Their Stress Reactions

We can also use Spielberger's model to understand how we may be able to help a person respond with less stressful reactions. In the model, there are two primary places where people can change their reactions to events. The first is in increasing one's coping skills. This can be done by such strategies as learning more about the things we find stressful, learning to relax, and learning to work more closely with others, as well as many other

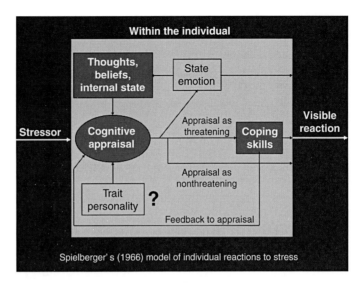

Figure 3.6. Spielberger Model f.

coping skills. This is supported by research which indicates that even a small amount of training in disaster response can reduce stress reactions in a disaster (Fig. 3.6).

We can also learn to monitor our thoughts and physical state (physical fitness and the level of tension in our bodies) to try to remain calm and positive. This can help us to make well-reasoned cognitive appraisals, and reduce unnecessary stress reactions. One tool for monitoring and controlling thoughts and our physical state is yoga. This technique has been practiced for thousands of years and can be very effective in helping us more consciously control our thoughts and physical state. There has been a large surge recently in "mindfulness meditation," which appears to be a repackaging of those ancient yoga techniques. Increasing our physical fitness can also improve our ability to effectively manage stress.

Another area in which we may be able to improve our cognitive appraisal is by focusing on our own belief systems. Many people have grown up holding beliefs that they learned as children, without ever critically examining whether they truly believe those things themselves. Many times our beliefs serve to put significant pressure on our cognitive appraisal. For example, if a man believes that male adults are supposed to be able to find places without asking directions, then losing his way on a family trip is much more stressful than if he believes that anyone can get off track. Similarly, if someone believes that they must "get it right" every time, it is much more stressful than if someone

believes that anyone can make a mistake. In sports, if you believe that your reputation is riding on whether or not you win,
it is much more stressful than if you believe that sports is just a
way to have some fun or get some exercise. *However, a word of
caution is needed.* Examining one's own beliefs is profitable, but
trying to challenge the beliefs of someone else may cause them
to reject your attempt to provide psychological support. Beliefs
often have strong emotions attached to them, and people can be
very defensive about their beliefs.

Reference

Spielberger, C. D. (1966). *Anxiety and behavior.* New York: Academic Press.

TRAUMATIC STRESS

PFA can be useful in helping people cope with everyday stress and daily hassles. But the particular importance of PFA is in supporting individuals who have experienced "traumatic (or overwhelming) stress." Most people can probably describe what stress is. But there is an entire chapter on traumatic stress in this book because, even though virtually everyone experiences some stress on a daily basis, people experience traumatic stress far less frequently. For this reason, people are usually not as familiar with responses to this more extreme form of stress. It can be very useful to recognize ordinary reactions to extraordinary events in others and in ourselves.

The defining characteristic of traumatic stress is that it can utterly overwhelm our coping skills, no matter how psychologically strong we are. Examples of traumatic experiences may include a significant personal assault, the sudden and unexpected death of a loved one, or the loss of all your possessions in a storm or fire. When someone's coping skills are overwhelmed by traumatic stress, we say they are experiencing a traumatic stress reaction. This is not a form of psychopathology or mental illness. It is simply an ordinary reaction to an extraordinary event. Traumatic stress reactions are not a sign of weakness, but a sign of being human.

Now someone might ask (and, indeed, many people have), "Is every reaction to a traumatic event an ordinary reaction?" In other words, "Is it possible to have a psychopathological response to a traumatic event, a response that is not ordinary?" Yes, there can be psychological responses to a traumatic event that are outside the normal range of human reactions and that represent genuine pathology. If you are going to provide PFA to people who have experienced traumatic stress, it is important for you to know the difference between ordinary responses to traumatic events and responses that may indicate that the individual needs a more professional form of psychological support.

This chapter will describe a range of ordinary reactions to traumatic events, and provide some idea of how to recognize responses that may require a consult with a trusted PFA provider, and/or possibly require a referral to a mental health professional. When and how to make a referral will be discussed in more detail in Chapter 11.

Generally, psychological reactions to traumatic events are described in four categories: emotional, physical, behavioral, and cognitive.

Emotional Reactions

The first and most widely known category of traumatic stress symptoms is emotions. It is important to realize that this discussion deals only with some of the more common emotions experienced in traumatic stress reactions. There may be many other emotions experienced in stress reactions. Moreover, each individual is likely to experience a unique combination of these emotions. There is no single characteristic pattern. Even a specific individual may experience different emotional reactions in response to different traumatic events.

Most people can readily identify fear and anxiety as common consequences of exposure to traumatic events, and indeed, these are perhaps the most common emotional reactions. But they certainly are not the only ones, and rarely occur in isolation. Sadness and even depression are also common experiences after traumatic events. Anger and irritability also frequently occur and may be particularly important because anger can affect one's responses and reactions to others quite dramatically.

There are also less common emotional reactions. Some individuals feel a lack of enjoyment in favorite activities or a lack of involvement in their routines. Some individuals feel a sense of emptiness or hopelessness about the future.

Another emotional reaction is feeling numb, withdrawn, or disconnected from people and events around the individual. It is important to realize that many people experience withdrawal and have no difficulty recovering from their traumatic stress reactions. But if this pattern of emotional reactions is different from the individual's feelings and behavior *before* the traumatic event, there is special reason to pay attention. A moderate body of research has indicated that these numbing/withdrawn emotions are often experienced by people who later have difficulties in working through their traumatic stress reactions. Therefore, when you are providing psychological support to someone who is feeling numb, or withdrawn, or disconnected, it is important to pay close attention to the needs of that individual and make sure that their reaction does not become worse. If this person continues to feel this way for 6 weeks, it would probably be a good idea to talk with another CBPFA provider or a mental health professional, and continuously assess whether this person might benefit from more traditional mental health services.

Physical Reactions

The second category of traumatic stress symptoms is physical reactions. Exposure to traumatic stress generally causes an arousal of the sympathetic portion of the autonomic nervous system. This produces many physical changes in the body, including increases in heart rate, blood pressure, and blood sugar. Many of those who experience traumatic events also experience other physical responses. Gastrointestinal problems (eg, stomach upset, nausea, diarrhea, cramps) may be the most common physical reaction, and these may also be related to the sympathetic arousal, which can interfere with the normal function of the gastrointestinal system. Sleep difficulties are also very common, including difficulty falling asleep, awakening during the night, and early morning awakening.

The physical reaction that might have the greatest consequence for people exposed to a traumatic event is suppression of the immune system, which can happen if someone experiences traumatic stress for a long period of time. The immune system protects the human body from infections of all kinds, destroying bacteria and viruses that enter the body. Some public health physicians have told me that following a major disaster they begin to plan for a wave of additional infectious diseases among those affected by the event a few months after it occurs. They assumed that this increase occurs because of the suppression of the immune system in many of those who were directly affected by the disaster.

In addition, oncologists (physicians who specialize in cancer) have told me that they believe that everyone probably develops cancer many times during their lives. In the great majority of cases, the immune system recognizes cancerous mutations of cells and quickly destroys them. When someone is diagnosed with cancer, according to these physicians, it is probably because the immune system for some reason has failed to perform its function.

Once the cancerous growth has reached a certain size, the immune system has difficulty combating it. A number of studies have reported that individuals diagnosed with cancer had experienced significant major stressors in their lives about 6 months prior to having their cancer diagnosed. (There are various scientific concerns with such research, but the studies raise questions about the possible role of traumatic experiences in making individuals more at risk for the development of cancer.)

Behavioral Reactions

The third category of common reactions to traumatic events is behavioral. This refers to changes in the way a person acts or behaves in the aftermath of a traumatic event. It is very common to see an increase in substance (alcohol or other drugs) use. Theorists often interpret this increase as an attempt to self-medicate the symptoms of traumatic stress reactions. Another behavioral change that is seen in the aftermath of traumatic events is an increase in family difficulties, including an increase in physical and emotional abuse of both children and spouses. This is probably partially a result of the increase in substance abuse, especially when coupled with increases in anger.

Ironically, another behavioral change that often occurs is that parents become *overprotective* of their families. This includes such things as parents refusing to allow family members to leave their sight, and this results in difficulty with family members going to work or attending school. As will be described more in Chapter 14, children may feel these concerns. It is also common for individuals to keep excessively busy. This is often interpreted as being an attempt to avoid intrusive memories. People may also find that they are very alert or easily startled.

Another behavioral reaction that needs particular attention from someone providing psychological support in the aftermath of a traumatic event is an individual isolating him/herself from others. If this is different from the individual's pre-event behavior, it may predict some difficulty in working through the traumatic stress reaction, just as with the emotional withdrawal mentioned previously.

Behavioral changes also include avoidance of places, activities, and people that bring back memories of the traumatic event. Although these behaviors may seem similar to the general emotional withdrawal and behavioral isolation described previously, these behaviors are specific to the traumatic event. Therefore, these are more likely to be reasonable reactions that constitute a potentially useful coping strategy, depending on how extreme the avoidance is. For example, someone who is mugged in a crime-ridden neighborhood may avoid passing through that neighborhood in the future. Such avoidance may be a wise decision to prevent future attacks. On the other hand, if the individual stops traveling outside their own immediate neighborhood, that could present a problem.

Cognitive Reactions

The fourth and final category of common reactions to traumatic stress is cognitive. Traumatic stress reactions affect our thinking, making it difficult to process information effectively. This commonly results in difficulty in concentration, problems in thinking clearly, difficulty in making decisions, difficulty with short-term memory, having unwanted memories that intrude into thoughts, having repeated unpleasant dreams or nightmares, and questioning spiritual/religious beliefs. This may be one of the most dangerous traumatic stress reactions.

Another cognitive reaction is a phenomenon known as a "flashback." This reaction seems to be unique to traumatic stress, so someone who has never before experienced traumatic stress may be shocked by the experience of a flashback. When a flashback occurs, the person feels like they are back in the moment of the original traumatic event. A flashback can vary with regard to how real it seems to the individual. The individual may actually see, hear, feel, smell, and even taste the same sensations that occurred during the original event. Some recent theory suggests that flashbacks may not always be a return to a specific event, but a blend of many previous difficult moments in life. Generally, flashbacks last 30 seconds or less. They usually become less frequent with time, but may occur periodically for years after the traumatic event.

People who do not know about flashbacks sometimes misinterpret these experiences as hallucinations and a sign that the person may be becoming psychotic. This is not the case. Flashbacks are classified as a form of dissociative disorder, which is not a psychotic process, but a form of stress reaction.

Over my decades of disaster response, probably the most powerful interventions I have done relate to flashbacks. Workers who are involved in the rescue and recovery process in mass casualty disasters have often approached me and whispered quietly to me concerns that they were becoming psychotic as a result of their work. Their quiet tones convey a deep fear of their reactions to the event. Such comments tell me very quickly what to expect as the conversation proceeds, but I always ask what leads them to think that they are becoming psychotic. Invariably, they reply that they have begun to have "hallucinations." I ask them to tell me about the hallucinations, and they tell me about having the sensation that they are back in the traumatic situation and everything seems real, as if it is happening again even though they have left the work site—it only lasts half a minute or so. When I explain to them that what they have experienced is not a hallucination, but a flashback, and that it is an ordinary reaction to an extraordinary event, they almost always offer an exclamation of relief. Then we have a longer discussion about managing the stress of such difficult work.

It should be noted, however, that people *can* have a psychotic reaction in response to a traumatic event, although that is extraordinarily rare. If in doubt, involve a mental health professional.

TRY THIS

Watch television news coverage of a natural or human-caused disaster or some significant tragic event. Observe the differences in the reactions of people shown in the video. Can you observe different emotions? Does everyone seem to be struggling to cope with the event, or are there some witnesses or onlookers who seem unaffected?

Individual Differences in Traumatic Stress Reactions

Different individuals are likely to have a wide variety of reactions to traumatic events. It would be extraordinarily rare to find someone who was experiencing the entire list of symptoms described previously. Each person tends to develop a fairly unique set of these symptoms. They may not have a symptom from every category (emotional, physical, behavioral, and cognitive), and sometimes people even experience some less common symptoms not described here.

There can also be real differences in how much time passes between the experience of a traumatic event and the beginning of traumatic stress reactions. Some people may begin to exhibit symptoms very soon after an event occurs. Others may initially have no symptoms, but first begin to have reactions such as those described previously months, and even more than a year later. When symptoms begin long after the event, people often have trouble even understanding that the symptoms are related to the traumatic event. They may even be fairly confused about why they are suddenly experiencing these difficulties.

CASE EXAMPLE

In one mass casualty incident, a psychologist spoke with a state police officer who had been providing security for the disaster-relief operation. The psychologist offered the officer information about how to receive free followup psychological care. The officer replied that he was not having any problems with coping and did not expect to have any. He told the psychologist that the officer was a long-time veteran of the state police and had managed many tragic traffic accidents, and was also a military combat veteran, so he was sure he would manage this event. The officer also said, however, that he genuinely appreciated the offer of support and had great respect for the importance of psychological support. The psychologist gave the officer the card with contact information anyway and told the officer that if he did experience any difficulties to just give a call. About 6 months later, the psychologist answered the phone and was surprised to hear the voice of that same state police officer. He sounded very upset, his voice shaking with emotion. He said he had experienced no problems since the end of the mass casualty operation until he woke up that morning. He said that "it had all come tumbling down on him" and said that he needed to talk to someone immediately, and would the psychologist see him if he came to his workplace. The psychologist offered to make a referral closer to where the officer lived, but the officer wanted to speak to someone who had been there. The psychologist told the officer that if he felt safe traveling, that he would see the officer when he arrived. The officer traveled some distance to the psychologist's office. When they talked, the officer again insisted that he had had no symptoms whatsoever in the intervening 6 months, but had been suddenly overwhelmed by the work at the disaster relief operation. Fortunately, some fairly simple therapy techniques (provided pro-bono; that is, without cost) helped the officer to work through the traumatic stress reaction. The officer had no explanation, however, for why the traumatic stress reaction had been delayed 6 months, and did not identify any trigger that may have brought on the reaction.

Different people can also experience their symptoms for different lengths of time, with or without good psychological support. Overall, individual differences mean that every person's experience of the event is unique.

When to Seek Professional Help

If there are so many ordinary variations in traumatic stress reactions, when is it time to suggest (or to seek out for oneself) the services of a mental health professional? We will explore this more in Chapter 11, but there are a few "rules of thumb" that are useful to remember. It may be time to seek some professional assistance when:

1. Unpleasant symptoms last more than 4–6 weeks, or
2. It becomes difficult to function effectively on the job, or at home, or at school, or
3. An individual feels concerned about his/her behaviors or emotions.

These are the guidelines I usually express to the public. As a provider, however, I would also suggest to you an extension of the second principle:

4. If you suspect that a person might pose a danger to him/herself or others, you need to make a formal referral to a mental health professional or if the danger seems imminent, to call 9-1-1 or otherwise contact law enforcement.

Similarly, I would suggest an extension to the third principle:

5. If you feel that the difficulties of someone you are supporting are uncomfortably beyond your skill level, it is important to make a referral to a mental health professional.

5

THE STRESS OF DISASTERS

What Makes One Disaster More Stressful Than Another?

Knowing the features that make one disaster more stressful than another and the characteristics of individuals that make them more susceptible to that stress may help to anticipate in which events people are more likely to need psychological support, and *which* individuals in that event may be more likely to require psychological support.

Characteristics of Events

These will be presented largely in telegraphic form, but entire books have been written on this topic. *Technological or human-caused disasters* (eg, transportation disasters, hazardous chemical spills, terrorist attacks) tend to be more stressful than natural disasters (eg, tornadoes, floods, hurricanes, earthquakes) for adults. (See Chapter 14 for information about children.) Many disasters, however, do not fit easily into one or the other category. Hurricane Katrina, for example, was clearly a natural disaster, but its impact was intensified drastically by human decisions. Heavy rains may cause flooding, but in some communities water has been released from reservoirs in order to protect homes above a dam, which results in flooding homes below that same dam. Is that flood below the dam a natural disaster or a human-caused disaster? An aviation disaster may be caused by sudden severe weather. Disasters are often a mix of natural and human-caused elements.

Disasters for which the *cause is unknown* are more stressful for adults. If people can identify a cause for an event, they are more likely to feel that they understand it. If they can understand it, they may feel more capable of dealing with the aftermath, preparing for the next time, or preventing a reoccurrence.

Disasters that occur without warning are generally more stressful than disasters that we know are coming. With advance knowledge, such as in a hurricane, people have the opportunity to prepare for the impact of the storm. In slow-rising floods, families have time to put furniture up above the anticipated floodwaters, and protect important papers and photographs.

This ability to prepare often gives people a sense of control over the disaster and reduces stress levels. Children can also prepare themselves for disaster if they have warning, but it is important not to presume that they have done so. For that matter, adults may not prepare even when they have the opportunity.

The duration of disasters is also significant—*disasters that last longer* are generally more stressful. This is another guideline that may be more difficult to interpret than you might think. An earthquake lasts only a few seconds. But aftershocks may go on for months afterward, and in massive earthquakes it may take years for the rubble to be cleared and even longer to rebuild if people choose to do so (and they usually do). In New Orleans after Hurricane Katrina, destroyed homes had barely begun to be cleared 7 months after the storm, and the huge majority of the population continued to live elsewhere in the United States. In North and South Dakota there are still counties heavily flooded from the storms and floods of 1993 and 1994. When does the disaster end?

It may be years before communities that experience an earthquake recover.
Photographer: Gerard Jacobs.

CASE EXAMPLE

Nepal experienced a significant earthquake in April 2015. I was asked to organize a Training of Trainers in CBPFA in Kathmandu, where 27 mental health professionals participated in the training. The training venue was atop a 10-story building. In the midst of the training, one afternoon an aftershock of moderate strength occurred. The strength of the earthquake was magnified by the height of the building, and the room where we were all located swayed significantly for some time. This aftershock was 7 months after the original earthquake. The participants sensed the quake immediately and rose with significant concern. It took me a few seconds before I sensed what was happening. We immediately broke from the training so that the participants could call friends and family to make sure they were okay. When did the Nepal earthquake end?

The *extent of the devastation* caused by a disaster is also a significant predictor of stress. If it is fairly easy for those directly affected by the disaster to get to an area that is unaffected and see neighborhoods that are "normal," the disaster is likely to be relatively less stressful than a disaster in which residents are constantly exposed to destruction and have difficulty returning to the normal routines of daily life. How much of the infrastructure needed to run the community is affected? Are government buildings still intact? Are water, electricity, and natural gas still functional? Are roads passable and bridges intact? Is public transportation still functional? To what degree can people live a normal life? Are grocery stores or hardware stores open? Are department stores open so that people can get fresh clothing and replace damaged objects? How much does the neighborhood still look like the neighborhood, the city still look like it did before the event?

A tornado may cause tremendous damage to a neighborhood, but leave most of the town untouched. On the other hand, a massive storm such as Hurricanes Sandy or Katrina or Andrew can cause severe damage across an extensive area or even a region. Survivors in the heart of the devastated area may have to travel great distances to escape scenes of destruction. Their cars may have been destroyed and public transportation may be unavailable, making it hard to get any sense of normalcy in their lives for quite some time. One woman living in a rural area in Mississippi when Hurricane Katrina struck told me that it was 2 weeks before anyone in her family were able to get out of the devastated area. In situations in which electricity has been disrupted and cars destroyed, it may even be difficult to learn the extent of the destruction caused by the disaster. Researchers studying the diaries of people who survived the massive 1906 earthquake in San Francisco noted that several of the survivors thought that the earthquake was the beginning of the biblical apocalypse, the end of the world. Without modern communications, and with everything they could see destroyed, they believed that the entire world had been destroyed.

The *number of deaths* in a disaster is also a significant predictor of the stress of a disaster. The *deaths of children* in an event increase the stress of the disaster dramatically. In communities with which I have worked throughout the world, horror at the death of a child seems to be a shared experience. We tend to believe that children are not supposed to die, and that parents should never have to bury their own child.

Some mental health professionals have told me that death would not matter to parents if their religion included a belief in reincarnation. Having worked with Hindu families who have had a child die in a disaster, I can tell you that such a notion is based on ignorance. Believing in reincarnation does not take away the pain of personal grief when a beloved child (or adult) dies. Christians may believe that if a loved one dies he or she goes to heaven and lives eternally in the presence of God. But that does not magically remove the personal pain of grief or the sorrow that the deceased loved one is no longer in the lives of the survivor.

The *postdisaster environment* is also a predictor of the stressful impact of an event. The sights, smells, and sounds that survivors of disasters encounter afterwards can increase the stress of a disaster event. The sight of devastated buildings, the sight and smell of dead bodies of livestock, and sadly sometimes of humans, the sounds of helicopters involved in rescue and recovery—all of these can increase the stress of the disaster experience. When Hurricane Floyd struck South Carolina in 1999, the extensive flooding that followed the enormous rainfall associated with the hurricane resulted in the deaths of hundreds of thousands of cattle and swine. In the lowland areas, where the carcasses were swept by the floodwaters, the stench was overwhelming and it took a very long time to destroy the animal carcasses and alleviate the stench. This greatly contributed to the stress of the event for the survivors and for the disaster relief workers.

The *management of the disaster relief operation* also has a strong influence on the stress of the disaster. If the public perceives that the response to an event has been poorly handled, regardless of the facts of the matter, it becomes more difficult to cope with the aftermath. Perceived failures in the response to Hurricane Katrina in New Orleans were headline news for months, which further aggravated an overwhelming disaster. On the other hand, a well-managed response serves to reduce the impact of a disaster. The smooth delivery of relief services leads people to believe that everything that can be done is being done to help them. This provides a soothing counterpoint to the losses in the event.

A related factor in the stress of an event is the *quality of communication by officials* during and after the event. People who have been exposed to a traumatic event often want to know all they can about the event as they struggle to comprehend what has happened to them and to their community. Keeping the public informed about developments in the event and in response to the event is extremely important. The anthrax terrorist attacks in the fall of 2001 were aggravated in some instances by government officials who gave extremely alarming press conferences, warning the public that handling their daily mail could result in their untimely death and the deaths of those whom they loved. This message was broadcast nationally, and many families throughout the country began to open their mail with rubber gloves, and many set aside a room or even a spot in their back yard to open the daily bills and letters.

New spokespersons replaced these alarmist officials who were raising fears. The revised message was that only a few pieces of mail in the entire nation had contained anthrax. Moreover, the pieces with anthrax and other pieces of mail contaminated by them were all from a few specific post office locations. Furthermore, they told the public, the entire matter concerned an extremely tiny percentage of the mail that passes through the United States in a single day. At that point, the alarm created by earlier spokespersons began to drop, and people's fears began to subside.

The type and intensity of *media coverage* also has a powerful influence on the stress of a disaster. In many ways the media needs to maintain a very difficult balance. They have the responsibility to communicate with the public regarding the event and the aftermath. Competition with other media sources pushes them to try to inform the public about developments as soon as possible. But they also have a responsibility to try to prevent unfounded rumors from being broadcast together with the facts and the official information regarding the event. Government officials have sometimes been accused of understating the damage from a disaster in order to calm the voters. On the other hand, officials have sometimes been accused of overstating the damage from a disaster in the hopes of securing more federal assistance. Similarly, media are sometimes accused of dramatically overstating disaster destruction to manufacture sensationalistic stories. But some of the documentaries about Katrina accused the media of not being diligent enough in the aftermath of the storm, and accused them of reporting conditions in the city based on what they could see from their hotel rooms in the French Quarter (which was relatively unaffected), unaware of the thousands of people trapped in their homes in the city as the flood waters rose after the storm.

I have heard both members of the public and disaster relief personnel complain bitterly about the aggressiveness of postdisaster media coverage, only to have those same people complain when the media departs the community, with residents asking sorrowfully, "Don't they care anymore?" In order to prevent overly enthusiastic media personnel from invading the privacy of grieving families at mass casualty disasters, I have supported preventing them from entering into family assistance centers where the families gather to await news about their loved ones. I have also, however, supported having media sites located immediately adjacent to these survivors areas, so that families who wish to speak to the media have the opportunity to leave the secured area and do so. Many disaster relief officials have learned that the best way to prevent overzealous journalism is to provide the media with official spokespersons who share as much accurate information as they can. This can be an effective strategy to undercut rumors.

It cannot be denied that the media have sometimes made poor choices about the television coverage of horrible events. These included live coverage of the bloodied bodies of dead babies being carried from the ruins of the Murrah Federal Office Building after the bombing in Oklahoma City in 1995, the broadcast of gruesome live images from the crash site of Flight 427 in Aliquippa PA in 1994, and the broadcast in the immediate aftermath of the September 11, 2001 attacks on the World Trade Center of individuals leaping to their death from the towers rather than be burned alive. In the latter case, responsible journalists and executives insisted that those images not be broadcast and it stopped. The point is that just because the media *can* broadcast something does not mean they *should* do so. The ethics involved in such situations are a matter of extensive debate within the journalistic professions.

Another aspect of the event that predicts how stressful an event will be is *whether families are separated* during the event. The separation of children from their parents, and even adult family members from one another can dramatically increase the stress of an event. This has lead to experienced disaster relief managers recommending to local disaster managers that they be sure not to separate families during evacuations. "Women and children first" may sound noble, but it is likely to result in a significant increase in stress levels for the families separated in such evacuations. Again this is an aspect of disaster that increased the stress of Hurricane Katrina, with many children winding up separated from their parents. It was reported that the last of the missing children was not reunited with their parents until months after the evacuation!

Finally, the *time and season of an event* can also influence the stressfulness for those affected. Disasters that occur at night are often more stressful, especially for children. There may also be less warning of storms that occur while families sleep. Similarly, the time of year may be significant. I have often heard disaster-response staff say that a winter flood is the most stressful type of disaster to work. Cold and wet seems to be much more stressful than merely wet.

Please note that this is not a comprehensive list of characteristics of events that may influence the stressfulness of the event. These are just a few of the stronger indicators that disaster-mental health staff use to predict how difficult a specific disaster is likely to be for those who are directly or indirectly affected.

Characteristics of Individuals

Just as the characteristics of an event predict how difficult the event will be, there are characteristics of individuals that predict, to an imperfect degree, how difficult an event will be for a specific person. Some of these factors are combinations of the event and the individual. For example, the *distance of the individual from the impact area* is an important piece of the picture of individual responses. Similarly, the *duration of exposure to the event* is important. It was probably far more stressful for residents of New Orleans who were stranded on interstate overpasses for days awaiting evacuation than for those who were able to flee before or immediately after the storm.

Another mixed indicator is the *reactions of other people* around the individual. If everyone around is being positive and collaborative and helping one another, the individual is likely to feel less stress than if there are many people angry or afraid or sad and openly expressing those emotions in outraged or boisterous behavior, or loudly crying and weeping. Panic in disasters is fairly rare, but when someone does panic, it is fairly likely that others will join in the panic.

The *degree of preparedness* of a family or individual also affects the stress of a disaster. The American Red Cross encourages the development of family disaster plans, and distributes brochures on how to develop such plans. Involving children in that process helps them to feel more prepared as well. In particularly disaster-prone areas, communities often encourage children in school to help develop a family disaster kit, or review an existing one to be sure that food, water, and other supplies such as batteries are fresh and ready to be used. This process of preparing as a family reduces the stress of events for everyone concerned.

TRY THIS

Contact the local chapter of the American Red Cross and ask them about printed information to help develop a family disaster plan. Follow the steps and help your family to be more prepared for disaster.

A *history of recent life stressors* can also make events more stressful. If you recall in Spielberger's model of individual reactions to stress, if someone is already anxious or angry or sad, they are more likely to appraise situations as threatening or irritating or depressing. Stress is additive. You may recall the old saying about "the straw that broke the camel's back." This saying is known all over the world. It refers to the ability of camels to carry extraordinary loads. But even the strongest camel, if loaded to its absolute limit, cannot carry a single straw more. Similarly, even individuals with extraordinary coping skills may accumulate stressful experience after stressful experience until the smallest stressor may cause them to have a severe stress reaction.

For this reason, individual/family characteristics such as recent major illness, the loss of a job, difficulties in school, or family conflict or divorce may cause individuals to be more susceptible to stressful events. Even if something such as a newly blended family has been a very positive experience for the family, it is likely to have used up some of the coping resources of the family and to make them more vulnerable. Similarly, having recently moved or immigrated into a community is likely to result in greater stress from a disaster. Even if that move has been mostly positive, or even wonderful, these individuals are likely to have used up some of their coping resources in dealing with the move, and are also likely to have fewer social supports in the community, and to have less understanding of the new community and how to recover within that community.

Long-term characteristics of individuals may also increase the stress of a disaster. A history of childhood traumatic experience, physical or sexual abuse, psychological problems such as psychiatric diagnoses or personality problems may result in a person appraising a disaster as more stressful than persons without these problems. Other characteristics such as poverty may also lead to a more stressful appraisal. Families and individuals with fewer economic resources to recover from the losses of a disaster are more likely to have difficulty. Being female also predicts a higher level of postevent stress. It is not clear whether events impact women more or if they are simply more likely than men to honestly report the stress they are experiencing.

There are other enduring characteristics that also influence stress reactions to events. Individuals who are members of ethnic minorities are more likely to experience stress than members of the majority. In the context of the aftermath of a disaster, feelings of alienation and discrimination are likely to be aggravated. There may be a perception of institutional racism (racial or ethnic prejudice that is manifested in biased policies and procedures which affect different groups in different ways) in the treatment of those affected and in the availability of services, whether that perceived racism is real or imagined. In Chapter 16, Dr Beth Boyd, one of the leading authorities in ethnic minority psychology, will address this in more detail.

Religion and culture can each have contradicting influences. Certainly many people draw strength from their religious beliefs and rituals. However, sometimes the beliefs of religions can make events more stressful for individuals who hold those beliefs. Some religions tell their members that God sent the event as punishment for their sins. In the aftermath of the December 26, 2004 Indian Ocean tsunami, I heard some Christian, Hindu, and Islamic leaders tell their followers that the tsunami was sent because of their sins. It is an enormous added burden to think that a quarter million people died and millions were left homeless because *YOU* sinned.

Cultural ceremonies can have a calming influence on people and bring comfort to them. The very participation in something familiar can return a sense of control. The Lakota people of South Dakota have purifying rituals to heal the mind and spirit. The Inipi or sweat ceremony is a physical, spiritual, and mental meditative journey guided by a spiritual leader. Another ceremony, the Sun Dance was actually outlawed for many years by the US government in an effort to force the Lakota people to be just like all the Christian Caucasians of Western European ancestry who dominated the nation at that time. The Sun Dance ceremony is also a blend of physical sacrifice, prayer, and community support to worship and ask for God's blessing. Individuals who participate may focus on their own spiritual and personal development and strength or may participate to support someone else in the community who is not at a point where they can participate in the physical rigors of the several-day ceremony. The community gathers in support of the dancers and it can be a growth and healing experience for all involved. In cultures throughout the world, I have found rituals that are performed to ease the transition through difficult times in life. The familiarity of the event itself and the social support provided by family, friends, and community are rich contributions of various cultural backgrounds.

How Stress Changes Through the Course of a Disaster

There are a number of models of how disasters evolve across time. The Red Cross promotes one of the more common models of the stages of disaster. The first stage is the "Heroic" phase, which begins shortly after the actual impact of the event. Commonly in the Heroic stage, there is a range of reactions. Some people are in a virtual (or actual) state of shock. More commonly, people exhibit heroic physical and/or psychological strength, engaging in extraordinary efforts to rescue people, or to mitigate (reduce) the impact of the event. An example of this latter behavior is the effort to prevent the flooding of Des Moines, Iowa in the Midwest floods of 1993. The people of Des Moines turned out in enormous numbers sandbagging along the river to try to save the city, and people came from all over the country to join in this successful effort. The length of the Heroic stage can be quite variable, but is generally no longer than a few days.

The Heroic phase tends to resolve into the "Honeymoon" phase. The most common psychological reactions during this phase involve feelings of relief at survival of the event and an appreciation of the enormous assistance effort that is typically fielded in the United States. One hears statements such as, "At least we survived; that's what's important," or "With all this help we'll be back to normal in no time." There is often an enhanced sense of community cohesion and camaraderie. Certainly there are people who do not participate in this elevated mood, who are suffering psychologically, but the community as a whole tends to feel good despite the horrible event that has occurred. The honeymoon phase is affected by many factors related to the event as described previously, including the quality of the disaster relief efforts, the degree of devastation of the infrastructure, and the numbers of deaths. This phase usually lasts from a few days to 2 weeks.

The honeymoon phase descends into the "Disillusionment" phase. This is the most difficult period in the aftermath of disaster. At this point people begin to realize the enormity of the event and the magnitude of their losses. The deaths of friends or family members or a family pet begin to become more real. People begin to consider losses that can never be replaced, such as family photographs. Although these losses may seem trivial to those who have not experienced them, the loss of things that help to form one's identity is difficult. Even the loss of a major tree or some similar element in the neighborhood or in one's yard can affect a family's "sense of place," the things that make a house or a community a home.

I recall a storm that swept through a very small town in South Dakota. The town had long been identified with the rows of very large and beautiful trees that lined both entrances to the town. In the storm, all the trees were destroyed. Although there was extensive damage to homes, people's focus was on the loss of the trees, both for their beauty and for fear of how it would change the identity of the town.

The entire roster of negative traumatic stress reactions described earlier in the book may appear during this phase. The general feel of communities in this phase of the aftermath of the disaster is the burden of the experience. Again, depending on the disaster and the disaster relief operation, the length of this phase may range from a week or two to a period of months. Some people have characterized the Hurricane Katrina disaster response as resulting in many months spent in the stage of disillusionment.

The most important challenge of disaster psychology is to help individuals and communities move from the phase of disillusionment to the "Recovery" or "Reconstruction" phase. People begin to enter into this phase when they begin to accept the losses they have suffered and to integrate those losses into a "new normal" life. People begin to make their new house or apartment their home. People get back to a pre-event job or find a new job if the old workplace has been destroyed. Children and adults begin to build new relationships in a new neighborhood, or adjust to the loss of neighbors. There are as many scenarios as there are people affected by the events. This phase may last months or years. It is common for this process to take more than a year, with the "new normal" only being reached after the 1-year anniversary of the event.

This is a very simple discussion of very complex processes in disaster. The stages do not necessarily flow one after another, and each person may move through the phases in their own individual time. Individuals may not be at the same phase as the overall community. The phases may leapfrog forward, and then backtrack to a previous phase. This discussion is intended to just give a rough idea of the processes involved in the movement from event to recovery.

6

ACTIVE LISTENING

Effective listening is the core skill of psychological support. People in cultures the world over seem to have a need to talk about their experiences when they live through a traumatic event. It seems to be a fairly universal human response, although it is expressed differently in various cultural contexts. The goal of CB-PFA is to let the individual know that there is someone who cares and is present to the individual to help work through this difficult time in the individual's life. That can largely and effectively be accomplished by being a good listener and by truly being present to the individual. CBPFA is *not* about doing therapy. CBPFA is *not* intended to heal psychopathology. The goal of CBPFA is *not* to help the person you are serving to reach some particular goal or to make some personality change, as might be the goal in psychotherapy. *It is important to remember that CBPFA is intended to support people who are experiencing an ordinary reaction to an extraordinary event in their lives.*

Community-Based Psychological First Aid. http://dx.doi.org/10.1016/B978-0-12-804292-2.00006-5

There is a set of skills known as "active listening" that is a very popular and scientifically validated approach to developing good listening skills, and is a core component of CBPFA. The great thing about being a good listener is that it can not only help you provide CBPFA more effectively but also develop or maintain quality interpersonal relationships in your personal life, at school, or at work. People who are good listeners are more likely to be hired, more likely to be promoted, and more likely to have strong interpersonal relationships, including romantic relationships. A study released a few years ago reported the results of a national survey of women's preferences in men. The most important feature in a romantic partner according to the women surveyed was to be a good listener. Active listening has benefits far beyond CBPFA. It is a life skill.

Many schools of psychotherapy consider active listening an important skill for therapists to use in serving their clients. Please note, however, that there are different levels of skill in active listening. Therapists in training may study active listening with a mentor for years to acquire the level of expertise in this skill needed to be an effective therapist, and may continue to work on that skill throughout their careers. But the basic seeds of this skill can be communicated fairly simply.

For several years, I have been teaching active listening using a model developed by Dr Beth Boyd, one of my colleagues in the Disaster Mental Health Institute. I have adapted that model a little with her permission.

The BESTT EARS Model

"Active listening" refers to the skills and attitudes that can help you provide support for someone by listening very effectively. In the doctoral Clinical Psychology Training Program, in which I have spent most of my career, we have a group of Lakota Native American elders who consult with us on cultural issues when we are working with students from a Lakota background, or when we are consulting with Lakota communities. This spirited group of consultants is known as the Council of Indigenous Advisors, and delight in referring to themselves as the "CIA." A few years ago we were planning a CBPFA training program for high school students primarily from Lakota communities, and we asked the CIA to meet with us and help us understand whether the community-based model of CBPFA would be appropriate in the Lakota context. When we described active listening, one of the elders said, "Oh – You mean you want them to be "Wawokiya." This was a term in the Lakota language with which I was unfamiliar, and I asked how it might be translated into English. They replied that this was a valued concept in the Lakota tradition, and basically meant one who "listens from the heart." I think that is a beautiful summary of the goal of active listening.

The word "active" in the name of this technique gives an important clue to this listening skill. If you want to be a good listener, it is not sufficient to sit passively while someone speaks to you. Carl Rogers was perhaps the most respected clinician in the United States for decades. He is often credited as the theorist most responsible for developing this technique. He suggested that the word "active" reflects both the task and the responsibility of the listener (Rogers & Farson, 1957). He also taught that listening takes place at many levels. In the *BESTT EARS* model, those levels have been grouped into two categories: nonverbal, and verbal.

The nonverbal areas to consider when you are listening include: *B*ody language, which can communicate your attention and support; *E*ye contact, which can show your respect and attention; *S*pace, including distance, position, and orientation; *T*ime, referring to a commitment to truly "be there" for the person you are supporting; and *T*ouch, which can be a tricky but powerful component. The first letters of these five areas form the first word of the active listening acronym: *BESTT*. The verbal areas to consider include: *E*ncourage; *A*sk questions, both to make sure you understand and to help the person you are supporting to understand his/her own thoughts and feelings; *R*estate/Reflect the story being told in your own words; and *S*ummarize, which is basically restating what the person has told you in your own words when the person is finished telling the story. These four areas of focus form the second part of the active-listening acronym: *EARS*. So the active listening acronym is *BESTT EARS*.

Cultural Considerations

Each of these topics listed in the previous paragraph will be considered in more detail. The significance of culture is an important factor throughout this discussion of active listening. Chapter 16 will address the topic of culture further, but its relevance in active listening requires mention in this discussion. An appropriate strategy in some cultural settings would be completely unacceptable in other cultures. Cultural variations will be noted in some discussions, but not all cultural variations can realistically be discussed in this context.

For each of the following suggestions, I want to be clear that I understand that some of these suggestions may be unacceptable either within your culture as the listener, or in the culture of the speaker. If you are providing support to someone who is from a culture other than your own, try to make sure that you practice behaviors that are culturally appropriate for you both. If you are in doubt about whether what you are doing is culturally comfortable for the one who is speaking, just ask the speaker. For example, "I will be listening to you carefully, because what you say is important to me. Please let me know if something I am doing is uncomfortable for you. I understand that the way I listen may be different from the way someone politely listens in your community, and I would appreciate it if you could give me suggestions of things that would help you feel more comfortable while talking to me."

People usually understand if someone who is not from their own culture does not understand the local customs. In many of the countries in which I have worked, people have been very understanding when I do something that is uncomfortable according to local customs. I try to study the cultures in which I work around the world, but there is only so much one can learn about a culture compared to someone who has grown up within that culture. Soon after coming to South Dakota, I was asked by a community agency to come to a rural Native American community that had experienced a terrible tragedy that resulted in the death of a young boy. I asked one of my doctoral students who himself was Native American to go with me. We worked with children in the school through the day, and in the evening held a town meeting. I fully expected that I would be challenged with regard to my knowledge of their culture. As predicted, the first person to speak was an elder, who forcefully challenged me, "What right do you have to come here and tell us how to grieve for our children?" I replied, "Absolutely none. And if your community had not asked me to come, I would not be here. I cannot tell you how to grieve for your children, but I *can* tell you how other communities have grieved, and you can decide for yourselves whether these techniques make sense for you." I went on to introduce my student, and pointed out that he was an enrolled member of a nearby related tribe. I told them that he had instructions to kick me every time I said something stupid, and that at the end of the day I was bruised but still standing. The elder nodded and sat down, and the meeting began. After the meeting, the elder sent me a message that I was welcome on the reservation whenever I chose to come. My willingness to admit my lack of understanding of the culture is what made my work there acceptable. Be comfortable asking for guidance if you are working with folks from cultures with which you are unfamiliar.

CASE EXAMPLE

Early in my work in South Dakota I was invited to teach a week-long course in stress management for the faculty of a Native American school on a reservation. I began the training by acknowledging my limited knowledge of their culture, and asked them to tell me if anything I said was in conflict with their traditions. The group looked at each other uncomfortably for a few moments. Then one of them stood and said, "This one time I will do this. What you ask is unacceptable because as the teacher of this course you are the elder in the room (although I was younger than any of the participants). It is rude in our culture to tell an elder that he or she is wrong." He then sat down. I thought about this for a moment and then said that even teachers can make mistakes and asked if it would be acceptable for them to tell me that it was time for me to become the student, and I would sit while they explained some relevant point in their culture. The participants gathered in a discussion circle for a few minutes, and then one of them stood and said, "This is acceptable." So several times through the week one of the participants would raise a hand and say, "It is time for you to become the student." I learned. They learned. And their culture was respected.

Nonverbal Aspects of Active Listening: BESTT

Body Language

Amazon, the commercial online bookseller, lists just over 111,000 books on body language (and that number has increased by 25,000 since I began writing this book). Some of the authors or publishers claim that reading their book will help you learn how to tell what a person is thinking by observing the person's body language. The problem with these amazing claims is that there is simply not scientific support for their claims other than, perhaps, facial expressions.

There is, however, scientific evidence for how people *interpret* the body language of other people. One commonly held belief is that arms crossed across the chest means that the individual is closed off from other people, or uninterested in what is going on. The truth is that if someone has crossed arms it may simply be because that position is comfortable for them, or the person is cold, or any number of things. It is best not to try to interpret body language.

But, remembering that people *do* interpret other people's body language, it is profitable to consider how other people may interpret *your* body language as you listen, and try not to communicate something other than what you intend. Try not to cross your arms. Holding your arms loosely with your hands in your lap generally communicates interest.

Try to be as relaxed as possible. If you feel nervous, you are likely to communicate that to the speaker, perhaps through very subtle physical cues, including muscle tension, fidgeting behavior, or rapid breathing. Playing with a pencil or pen, particularly if you are tapping the pen on a desk or table, can be distracting to the speaker and lead to a conclusion that you are not interested in what is being said. Try not to drum your fingers, tap your foot, or perform other nervous habits.

On the other hand if you are relaxed and comfortable you will probably communicate that subtly as well. Try to have a calm facial expression. Try to sit as calmly as you can. I know that a person cannot just turn a switch and stop being nervous, but as you practice active listening and become more experienced and more comfortable with the process, you will probably learn to sense your unnecessary tension and release it.

Eye Contact

In mainstream culture in the United States, eye contact is expected. Your attention communicates respect. Maintaining eye contact also helps you as the listener to maintain your focus on the speaker. It is not, however, a staring contest. Try to casually maintain eye contact.

This is one of the aspects of active listening that is culture bound. There are some cultures in which eye contact is considered rude. For example, in traditional Lakota culture, eye contact with an elder is considered disrespectful. If you choose to provide psychological support to someone who is from a culture different from your own, it is important to try to learn about that person's cultural background and worldview.

Space

The "space" component of nonverbal aspects of active listening includes three subcomponents: Position, Orientation, and Distance (POD).

Position

The position subcomponent of *Space* is fairly simple. If you want to speak with someone in providing PFA, try to match his/her position. If the person is standing, stand to listen to her/him. If the person is sitting (and cultural protocol does not require that you stand in the person's presence) then sit to listen. People are generally more comfortable when the person with whom they are talking matches the speaker's position.

Position and Distance are important when having a discussion. Photographer: Gerard Jacobs.

Orientation

Orientation refers to how one's body is turned. In mainstream US society, people generally expect the listener to directly face the speaker, or nearly so. But this subcomponent is also culture bound. There are some cultures and some religious groups that have specific expectations with regard to orientation.

I would like to believe that I am fairly observant, and that I am rather attentive to cultural issues. However, I was recently talking with a colleague in a Lakota community. We were part of a fairly large group in a meeting room, and people had paired off in having discussions. I drew up my chair facing my colleague, and he shook his head and said to me, "You should really know this by now. (I have been working in Lakota communities for more than a quarter century.) But since you do not seem to have learned it on your own, I will tell you. In the Lakota culture, when we are having a discussion, we sit with our chairs parallel and sit facing the same direction while we talk." I looked around the room, and everyone else was, indeed, talking while sitting with shoulders parallel, facing the same direction. I felt fairly stupid, but I was grateful that my colleague had finally pointed out what I had missed for decades.

I have been in countries in which it was considered rude to have your feet or your knees pointed toward the person with whom you were speaking, whether you were sitting or standing. In at least one country, it was important to point your toes a little to one side, but there was still an expectation of having your torso directly facing the person with whom you were speaking. I found that physically uncomfortable, but I did so, because it was the cultural expectation. A related issue is that a number of cultures find it offensive if a person allows the soles of their feet/shoes to be seen.

Distance

Each person has a space that the individual considers private. This concept is referred to in psychology as "personal space." If we could magically make personal space visible, we would see everyone surrounded by a bubble. Each person's bubble might be a little different in size, and the size of people's personal space from different cultures may be very different in size. If someone else breaks that bubble by coming too close to us, we feel uncomfortable, unless that person is a friend or a loved one. Most people find that they are comfortable with family members and good friends being closer to us than people we know less well, or for whom we have less affection. Perhaps this is the origin of the expression "close friend."

Ohio University had many foreign national students when I taught there about 30 years ago. After a while, I got to know where students were from by where they stood when they came into my office. Personal space in the United States is probably about average among the cultures of the world, although it differs somewhat from place to place even within the United States. In some countries, personal space is much smaller. People in these countries are comfortable standing in very close proximity, even touching chests as they talk. There are other countries in which personal space is considered very large for people whom you respect. Some students would come to see me and stand at the door to talk to me, not even entering the office. (My desk was about 10 ft. from the door.) Other students would enter my office and actually lean across my desk to talk to me. It was amazingly variable, yet predictable based on the student's cultural background.

In my experience in the United States, when a large number of people want to do something such as buy a ticket at a theater, they form a line and generally are rather orderly waiting their turns. I was surprised the first time I needed to do this in another country where I was traveling. Everyone who needed to get assistance from a clerk working behind a window simply crowded forward, pushing and shoving to gain position. There was no line. It was very surprising to me, but was obviously not unusual to anyone in the crowd except me. Their personal space was much smaller than mine.

On one of my first trips overseas, I stepped into an elevator, and someone said loudly in English, "American on board!" I was curious enough that I decided to ask how he knew. He told me that Americans tend to assume the "elevator position" when they enter an elevator. He said Americans tend to turn, face the front of the elevator, cross their hands in front of their genitals, and look down. I had never been aware of it before, but that was exactly how I had stood. The man told me that he thought Americans did that because they have a much larger personal space than residents from other cultures. He told me that he imagined that people in the elevator position were silently saying to themselves, "This is not happening. My personal space is not being violated." Since that experience, I have paid attention when elevator doors open in the United States, and it is amusing to me how many times people are, indeed, standing in the elevator position.

Orientation and distance may differ in various cultural contexts. Photographer: Gerard Jacobs.

When you are providing psychological support to someone, try to be aware of his/her reaction as you approach her/him. If the person moves a little further away from you, it is profitable not to approach closer. Give the individual her/his space. As trust grows between you, it may be reasonable to approach closer. But if you begin by approaching too close, it is liable to result in a rejection of your offer of support.

Time

One of the critical factors in active listening is to make a commitment to spend the time needed to provide the individual with good psychological support. From my perspective, when you ask someone, "How are you doing?" or "How are you?" it is best for that question to be a sincere one.

A colleague was recently walking past me and appeared distressed. I asked as she passed how she was doing. She replied automatically, "Fine," and continued past me. A few feet past me she stopped, turned around, and said, "You were serious, weren't you?" I replied that I was, and she turned and told me about what a rough morning it had been. She only spoke for a few minutes before telling me she had to get to a meeting, but thanked me, saying that it really helped to share her difficulties with someone. From my perspective, this was a good example of PFA. When I asked her how she was, I knew that my question might involve a commitment of time.

Years ago, I heard a presentation by a spiritual leader describing the importance of "being present" to someone. I was fascinated by the discussion, and began to think about the concept quite a bit. It was in disaster psychology that I began to see the tremendous importance of providing support simply by being there for someone to share some of the experience of the traumatic event. In the American Red Cross disaster response to the crash of Flight 427 outside Pittsburgh in 1994, one of those directing the recovery effort at the crash site asked that we position psychological support staff at the recovery site. I agreed, but because of national standards, we positioned our team outside the inner perimeter, which surrounds the area where the actual recovery work was being done. We positioned ourselves at the entry/exit points of the inner perimeter. I told our staff, all mental health professionals, not to expect the recovery personnel to speak to us as they came out of the inner perimeter. I asked everyone to be clearly identified as mental health professionals, and to simply help the workers with water and food, or in removing or getting into their biohazard gear. If the workers wanted to talk to us, it was important that they initiate the discussion, because it was important for them to maintain their defenses. They had to go back into the inner perimeter repeatedly for days, and letting down their defenses could disable their effectiveness. Indeed, very few of the workers spoke with us at the crash site. When the recovery was declared over, however, and they knew they would not have to go back into that horrendous site, many of the workers approached one or another of our mental health team. They all said much the same thing: "I didn't talk to you up on the hill (where the crash site was located) and I'm not going to talk to you now. But you will never know what it meant to see you there every time I walked up out of that (expletive deleted) hole (the aircraft had formed a crater in the hill when it crashed) and know that you were there just to support me." Since that time, disaster mental health staff have heard such things many times from recovery personnel. The psychological support was provided simply by our presence, being present to them, making the commitment of time.

After the 1994 Indian Ocean tsunami, a disaster that resulted in the deaths of more people than any other in recorded history, I was asked by the International Union of Psychological Science to organize a training of psychologists and some other mental health professionals from the most affected countries. At the training, the head of the group from Thailand asked to make a presentation on their Buddhist approach to disaster psychology. Basically,

Just "being there" for someone can be powerful psychological support.
Photographer: Burak Aydin

he said that they move into the affected area, search for individuals affected by the event, and then sit down next to them in total silence; not even introducing themselves. When they decide that the individual feels better, they get up and move on to the next person. That is a bit more reliance on being present to them than I would advocate, but I think it illustrates the importance that mental health professionals attach to this strategy.

Touch

The original version of this teaching strategy for active listening did not include touch. Although this gave a better acronym, I think that touch is important enough to warrant misspelling "best" by adding an extra "t." Touch is one of the most powerful forms of communication known to human beings. It can be a very powerful tool, but it can also be damaging if it is done poorly or is significantly misinterpreted. Touch can be misinterpreted as a sexual advance, and result in great harm, even though the person touching intended nothing but psychological support.

A touch on the arm, or a gentle pat on the back is generally considered fairly safe among my colleagues. But even with such touch, it is important to remember that there are significant cultural factors regarding touch. Some cultures and religions forbid touch between adults of opposite genders unless the two people are biologically related or related by marriage.

In psychology, physical touch beyond a handshake between therapist and client is generally discouraged. Therefore, I had been very cautious about touch throughout my professional life up until the time I responded to my first mass casualty event. To my surprise, a large percentage of the survivors and family members would frequently just walk up and hug those involved in the disaster response. In the many disaster relief operations in which I have worked, this has been common. So, as strange as it initially seemed to me, I have gotten used to it. Moreover, among frequent responders in American Red Cross Disaster Services, it is very common to greet one another with a hug. But even though hugs are common in these settings, I recommend that even there people ask before giving someone a hug. Asking permission can help to ensure that when we think someone needs a hug, it is not really that *we* feel a need to *give* a hug. Asking can also help reduce the possibility of misinterpretation of the touch. The American Red Cross formally recommended "sidal hugs" at one point, standing with shoulders parallel side by side, extending an arm around the person's back and squeezing the far shoulder. I have honestly never known someone who wanted a hug to find a sidal hug satisfying.

CASE EXAMPLE

Beyond cultural issues, there are also individual differences in touch. I have known a woman for many years. She is very kind and highly respected in her church community. She is a leader in many of the church's activities for children. She is intelligent and well-educated. She has an excellent personality. She also despises being touched... at all... by anyone. We have stayed in touch for many years, but I do not have the opportunity to visit very often. When I do, I sometimes forget her aversion to touch, and hug her on greeting, which I do typically with family and friends. When I make this error, I feel her go absolutely stiff. I step back and apologize. Thankfully, she has forgiven me immediately each time. The important point is that ordinary people in mainstream US culture may not want to be touched at all, regardless of the intent of the touch.

In CBPFA, you will most frequently be supporting family and friends, so some of these cautions may be less of a concern. But I encourage you to use touch cautiously and with careful consideration.

Conclusions

So I encourage you to be aware of your body language, to make appropriate eye contact, to be thoughtful about space issues, to commit yourself to spend the time needed to help, and to use touch cautiously. Listen as *BESTT* you can.

Verbal Aspects of Active Listening: EARS

Some people find it strange that good *listening* requires verbal behavior. But remember that the technique for being a good listener is *active*. It is not enough to sit or stand like a statue in front of the speaker. When many typical social conversations take place, the process is highly interactive. It is common for people to challenge one another's perspectives and decisions, and it is common for those participating to feel the need to defend their point of view or actions they have taken. In contrast, Rogers maintained that the open attitude of the listener and absence of judging the speaker in active listening helps the speaker to feel less defensive and creates a supportive environment in which the individual can explore his/her own potential solutions. Nevertheless, there are a few verbal tools that can improve the effectiveness of the listening.

As you listen, it is useful to make sure that you understand the story of the event that the speaker is describing to you. It is not important whether you feel that the story is accurate or whether you think the speaker made appropriate decisions, only that you understand the speaker's perspective. A few techniques for helping to accomplish this will be described subsequently.

Encourage

Many theoretical schools encourage therapists to be neutral in the relationship with the client. There are various reasons for those theories, but therapy often has longer-term grander-scale goals than does CBPFA. In active listening within the context of CBPFA, I recommend that you be openly supporting and encouraging. CBPFA does not seek to create a therapeutic environment, but an overtly supportive one.

Maintain a pleasant tone of voice and choose soothing words. One of the strange features of my education is that my undergraduate degree is a dual degree in ancient Greek and Latin. The reason is simple: the university offered to help pay my way through college if I would major in those topics. I had occasionally heard of ancient Greek "soothsayers" in my high school years. Texts suggested that these had been similar to modern day fortunetellers, and indeed *Word's* dictionary tool defines the word as a fortuneteller. In studying ancient Greek culture, however, a different picture emerged. The soothsayers tended to have their locations near natural hot springs and steam vents outside various cities. People of power and wealth, stressed by the difficulties of daily business would go out to the soothsayers for what we might think of now as a "spa day." The stressed clients would take a steam bath or a hot mineral bath, and often be massaged (and perhaps offered some drugs) as they told their troubles to the soothsayer, who would, in turn, say soothing words—that is be a soothing sayer. Imagine the stressed client laying on a table, relaxing, as the soothsayer massaged the client's tense shoulders, saying, "There, there. Things will be better tomorrow." Note that I am not suggesting you administer drugs or give the person you are supporting a massage or a steam bath, although the latter points may be useful if you are supporting a spouse or personal partner.

Some researchers suggest that a lower tone of voice is more soothing. I find it interesting that people often speak to infants in a very high-pitched voice. Some researchers have indicated that higher pitches are actually irritating to infants, which is why they tend to respond more, but you may get a better long-term positive reaction by speaking in low soothing voice. The same tends to be true for adults.

There are also some nonverbal cues that can be soothing in your active listening, although they are often classified together with verbal aspects of listening. Giving encouraging head prompts will often result in a person telling you their story in more detail. Slight head nods, together with verbal utterances such as, "Mm-hmm" or "Uh-huh" can also be useful in helping a speaker to feel supported as she/he tells the story.

Interestingly, even these verbal prompts and head nods may differ from culture to culture. When I was a visiting professor in Santiago de Compostela in Spain, one of the cultural differences that seemed strange to me was the use of very different verbal prompts, and in Bulgaria, head nods and shaking one's head had the opposite meaning that they have in the United States. Using culturally appropriate head prompts and verbal utterances can demonstrate to the speaker that you are following what the person is saying, that you are interested, and that you are encouraging the speaker to continue.

Ask Questions

Asking questions can effectively serve two purposes. First, asking questions can help you make sure that you understand the story the speaker is telling. Second, asking questions can also help the speaker clarify and understand his/her own thoughts and feelings experienced during the event.

One important principle of active listening is to try not to interrupt as the speaker tells the story. If you have a question or want to clarify something, wait until the speaker pauses or has finished telling his/her story. But remember that active listening means that you are not simply sitting quietly and letting your mind wander. You need to actively focus on the speaker's narrative of the events and develop an understanding of her/his story.

Increasing Your Understanding

Asking questions about the speaker's story to clarify your understanding provides evidence that the listener is focused on the speaker. But try to hold those questions until the speaker pauses in the story. Do not jump in the instant the speaker takes a breath. Try to be calm and deliberate.

If I am listening to someone as I try to provide psychological support in a disaster, I will often use a note pad and jot down brief questions. If the speaker seems curious about what I am doing, I explain that I do not trust my memory and that the speaker's story is important to me, so I did not want to interrupt, but I wanted to remember questions to ask when the speaker was finished telling the story. Then I show him/her the notepad—no secrets, no mysteries. And, of course, I do not write anything on that notepad except questions for that specific discussion. Some of my colleagues think that the use of a notepad to remember questions is a terrible technique, but in more than 30 years as a psychologist, I am not aware of anyone ever taking offense at it. I think most people's memories are fallible, and they understand the need to take a note now and then. It also provides evidence that what they have to say really is important to me. This can also help you to wait to ask your questions until the speaker has finished. Just be sure not to doodle or spend too much time writing. Also, be sure to destroy your notes after the conversation.

Avoid asking, "Why?" and "Why not?" Such statements are often seen as judgmental and may be seen as threatening by the speaker. Be sure to avoid judging the quality of the speaker's reactions both in the event and in the time since the event. CBPFA is not a time to be judging the person you are trying to support.

Aiding the Speaker's Understanding

Ask questions about the speaker's feelings and thoughts. I referred earlier to the fact there seems to be a universal need for humans to talk about their experience after experiencing a traumatic event, even in cultures in which it is generally unacceptable to talk about one's own difficulties. It seems likely people have that need, in part, to try to understand their own reactions by telling their story. Remember that traumatic stress can make it difficult to think clearly. Therefore, questions such as, "What were you thinking as that was happening?" or "That must have been overwhelming. What were you feeling?" can be helpful to the speaker, and give them an opportunity to reflect on his/her experience.

Restate/Reflect

When the speaker pauses, it may be a good idea to occasionally restate a part of the story in your own words to make sure you understand. This is a technique called "reflection." It is an effective technique for demonstrating that you have been listening, and that you understand the speaker's perspective on the events. It also helps you to be sure that you really do understand the perspective of the speaker. Be open to having the speaker correct some aspect of your telling of the speaker's story. You may even be certain that you are correct in reflecting what the speaker originally said. But that is not important. Accept the correction and allow the story to go on. My wife and I have been married for more than 40 years, and she can tell you that she still needs to correct me sometimes when I use reflection to summarize the story she has told me.

It is especially important that you use your own words in restating what the speaker has said. When a listener simply repeats the speaker's words, it is called "parroting." Parroting can lead the speaker to feel that the listener is mocking him/her. It can create negative feelings that can significantly interfere with the openness that is an important point in active listening. If a client tells you about his/her experiences in the event and concludes with, "I feel sad," and you respond, "You feel sad," it does not tell the client that you understand the client's experience. A tape recorder could do the same thing. But if the client tells you that same thing and you respond, "That must have been a very difficult experience. It would amaze me if you did not feel sad," the client will understand that you "get" their experience, and will therefore be likely to share more of their story with you.

Summarize

As you listen, you need to make sure that you are understanding the story of the event that the speaker is describing to you. It is not important whether you feel that the story is accurate or whether you think the speaker made appropriate decisions. For purposes of active listening, it is only important that you understand the speaker's perspective. When the speaker completes the story, summarizing that story as you understand it and in your own words provides an opportunity to make sure you got the story right. It also provides evidence for the speaker that you made the effort to get the story right. Essentially, this is the same process as reflection, described in the previous step, but performed after the story is completed.

Other Verbal Suggestions

There are a few other notes to consider, which are not strictly part of active listening, but important to consider in your verbal comments. Avoid statements such as, "I know how you feel." I have often heard people say this phrase in trying to show their compassion for someone. Without exception, people have responded to this statement with resentment, and occasionally with outright anger. People generally do not feel that *any* listener can truly understand how the speaker feels, particularly if the speaker has suffered significant losses. In general, there are many things that people say in trying to comfort others that have the opposite effect.

My father had two signs that hung above his workbench. One said, "Even a bass wouldn't get in trouble if he kept his mouth shut," and it featured a bass leaping out of the water with a fishing lure hooked in its mouth. The other now hangs above my workbench. It said, simply, "Engage brain before putting mouth in gear." I encourage you to think carefully before you speak. Do not be in a hurry to say something. Be certain your words intended to support actually do so. Try to make certain that you do not judge the person's experience or reactions in the event or since the event.

Emotional Aspects of Listening

Active listening can be a very powerful component of psychological support. But it is only effective as long as the listener matches what she/he says with how the listener feels. If the listener is thinking, "This person deserves what they got," but says something very caring and supportive, the speaker is likely to pick up on the conflict in the listener. The speaker may not know exactly why, but is likely to have less trust in the listener, and consequently the active listening will be less effective.

Having a calm and caring presence to the speaker means genuinely feeling calm and caring. Although you may have a very different feeling about the event than what the speaker is describing, or may have different values than those being expressed by the speaker, it is important to allow the speaker to be who he/she is. If you come into the conversation with preconceived notions about the individual, it will be much more difficult to provide psychological support. Therefore, it is important to reach a personal feeling of peace and calmness as much as you can before beginning the process.

In a similar vein, Carl Rogers talked about the importance of another quality in active listening: congruence. Although a great deal could be (and indeed has been) written about this concept, the basic strategy that Rogers was trying to promote was that the listener needed to really be him/herself. Be true to who you are. People seem to be able to tell if you are being fake, and the speaker is not likely to feel supported if you only *act* as if you care.

Cognitive Aspects of Listening

A critically important step in active listening is to have a mindset that will help you to focus intently on the speaker. One cannot listen effectively if one is silently thinking about what to buy later at the grocery, or about an argument with someone earlier in the day, or if you are thinking about what you want to say to the speaker to make your point or give a contrasting perspective. It is important to try to quiet your own thoughts so that you can focus on what the speaker is saying, that is, to truly be present in the moment. Rogers proposed that when a speaker is listened to intently she/he becomes more open to his/her own experience and focuses on her/his own challenges, resources, and perspectives more realistically (Rogers & Farson, 1957). These benefits contribute to more effective problem-solving efforts. Problem-solving will be addressed in Chapter 7.

Closing Thoughts on Active Listening

Finally, remember that no matter how you personally view an event, if the individual you are serving sees an event as traumatic, then it is—at least for that individual. Sometimes people will experience an event as traumatic that you may not see in the same way. It does not help to tell the speaker that the event was not so bad, or could have been worse. This will only serve to judge the speaker's response and invalidate the speaker's reactions to the event. That is not good psychological support. People most often offer this kind of judgmental reaction to children who experience an event as traumatic. It is often difficult for adults to truly understand the world from a child's perspective. It is enough, however, to accept that if the child experiences something as traumatic, then for them it *is* traumatic.

I remember working with one law-enforcement officer who felt overwhelmed by a difficult disaster. With just a little psychological support he was able to cope effectively. His one major question, however, was why this event had affected him so significantly, when he had no such reactions to many other difficult events. That answer I could not give him. I assured him that it was only important for him to realize that this event *was* traumatic for him, regardless of the reason, and that he had learned how to cope with it.

If you want to provide someone with good psychological support, make an effort to listen to him/her effectively. The *BESTT EARS* model is the best strategy I know for doing that. As I will try to demonstrate in the Chapter 7, *BESTT EARS* is also an integral part of effective problem-solving.

TRY THIS

Tell someone with whom you feel safe that you are trying to be a better listener and would like to practice your listening skills in your conversations with that person in the coming week. Then try out the *BESTT EARS* technique. Review the steps in the *BESTT EARS* model between conversations, and see how comfortable you can become with these skills.

Reference

Rogers, C. R., & Larson, R. E. (1957). *Active listening.* Chicago: University of Chicago.

7

PROBLEM-SOLVING

After you have provided active listening, you are likely to have a better idea of what the person you are supporting may need or with which he/she may be struggling. As the client tells you their story, and you get a better understanding of the challenges they may be confronting, you may be able to provide support by helping the person to develop solutions for some of the problems that are resulting in continuing stress.

One of the popular models for problem-solving was adapted and has been promoted by Dr Teresa Lafromboise (1996). The model uses the acronym "*SODA*," for *Stop, Options, Decide, Act.* In my work, I have long believed that it is important to add an additional formal step to the model: *Evaluate*. I know, I know. That ruins the cute acronym, but as I will explain, I think that step is important enough to have its own letter.

Stop

The first part of the acronym, *Stop,* is by far the lengthiest. In physical first aid, the American Red Cross similarly advises that before approaching someone whom you believe needs first aid, it is important to stop and assess the situation. Every year, it seems, I come across a news story about a helper rushing into a situation to assist someone in need, and instead winding up a casualty him/herself. It is important to assess the situation before rushing in, to be as certain as possible of the appropriate next step. The same is true in CBPFA. One of the founders of disaster mental health, Dr Robert (Bob) Hayes, has been well known for his advice to beginning mental health professionals, "Don't just do something, stand there." People hearing this often at first hear it as the adage, "Don't just stand there..." The point that Hayes was making, was that it is important to stop and assess the situation before you rush in and begin to try to help. It is important to understand what needs to be done before you start trying to do it, and it is important to make sure that *you* are ready before you leap into the effort.

This *Stop* portion of the acronym is divided into several steps. One of my doctoral students, Ms Amanda Reed developed an acronym to help remember these steps: *Be A BUD*. This stands for *be aware of your own stress, assess the situation, build the relationship, understand concerns*, and *define/identify the problem*. Each of these steps will be discussed subsequently.

Stop—Be Aware of Your Own Stress

It is useful to take a moment to gather yourself before beginning. "Freaking out" does not help anyone. It is very useful to calm yourself before reaching out to someone whom you wish to support. That does not mean that it is wrong to feel emotional as you are listening to people tell you their stories. Sometimes you may even find the story someone is telling you to be overwhelming. Certainly, I have often felt overwhelmed when working in a mass-casualty incident. In response, I would try to take a moment to remember my role, and that this moment was not the time for me to experience my own stress response. It can significantly distract from your efforts to provide CBPFA if you are experiencing intense reactions yourself. On the other hand, I have definitely shared tears with some of the people whom I have supported.

Someone (I will refer to him as Dave) recently told me of an experience related to this point. Dave had received a call from a friend of his (whom I will refer to as Jim). Jim was a fairly young man who, like many men in our society, did not like going to a physician when he was feeling bad. But Jim had been experiencing increasingly problematic physical symptoms, and after months of problems, finally went to see his physician. Unfortunately, Jim discovered that he had end-stage cancer. It was a fast-growing type, and had spread significantly in his body. The physician had told Jim that there was no practical way to treat his condition, and that

Jim had only a very short time to live. Dave said that he rushed to the hospital to visit his dying friend after learning of the diagnosis. But when he got to Jim's hospital room, he found himself so upset at the thought of his friend Jim dying, that Jim, the man dealing with cancer, actually wound up comforting Dave, the visitor, during most of the visit. Dave told me that when he left the hospital, he was very disappointed with himself, and wished that he had taken the time to calm and compose himself before going to visit Jim, so that he could have been genuinely supportive of his friend who was facing death.

Do Not Worry About Whom to Blame

It is a fairly common experience to want to find someone to blame when a terrible event happens. Sometimes we feel better for a few moments if we can focus our anger and/or disappointment on some person or agency or group to whom we can assign (rightly or wrongly) responsibility for everything that has gone wrong. But blame does not tend to be very useful for very long. Intense negative feelings can become even worse when someone has a target for those feelings. Expressing your anger toward a target can actually increase your anger. Therefore, do not try to tell the person whom you are supporting who or what organization you think they should blame, and do not try to figure out for yourself whom to blame. It is not a profitable investment of energy.

Take Responsibility for Things for Which You Really Are Responsible

Let me begin this discussion with a major caveat: I am not suggesting that you place yourself in any legal jeopardy. But sometimes someone in distress will decide to place some blame on whoever is around. And if you are supporting friends and family, it may be that you have been involved in their lives to some extent. So the person you are supporting may say, "This is all your fault." If it is true that you share responsibility for the event to some extent, it can be useful to not be defensive. Sometimes it can be useful to reply to such accusations by saying something such as, "Well, if I'm responsible in some way, I'm sorry, but let's figure out how we can best proceed from here."

STOP—Assess the Situation

Once you have made sure you can proceed in a composed manner, it is time to determine what information you need to solve the problem. This is an extremely important part of problem-solving.

What information do you need to help solve the problem? It is useful to understand a problem well before trying to support someone in developing a solution to the target problem.

First, what happened? Having responded to disasters of many different kinds in many parts of the world, I have been struck at how many different stories there are about what happened in each event. The rumor mill typically has explanations from the sublime to the ridiculous. This is true even in fairly simple events. If you are providing support to someone, it is most important to understand the perspective of the person whom you are supporting. This is far more important than understanding the official story. This magnifies the importance of listening very carefully to the individual's story before attempting problem-solving; to use the *BESTT EARS* technique to maximum advantage.

Photographer: Gerard Jacobs.

Second, how dangerous is the situation? In disaster-mental health operations I have always tried to send professionals out to work in the community in mixed-gender pairs. This is done partially to improve the team's ability to provide psychological support, because some people prefer to talk to a woman, and others prefer to talk to a man. (By the way, it is not as simple as men prefer to talk to one gender, and women the other.) But, deploying teams rather than individuals also increases the safety of the workers, whether the teams are mixed gender or not.

There are some problems that may present genuine danger to anyone getting involved. I recently saw news coverage of a group of houses that were endangered by severe erosion that had undermined the cliff along which the houses were built. As the news team filmed, an owner of one of the houses was appealing to the onlookers to rush in and help save at least some possessions from the house. As the owner was pleading, the house toppled over the cliff and plummeted to the ground, completely shattering. To me it seemed likely that anyone who had rushed in to help the owner would have died when it fell. Thankfully, the onlookers had seen the potential danger and did not attempt to come to the owner's aid. It was not that they did not care. They had stopped, assessed the situation, and probably determined that it was just too dangerous.

One of the most common dangers that you may encounter in providing CBPFA is domestic violence. If you know that someone you are supporting or intend to support has been coping with domestic violence, it is important to realize the danger that may be involved *for you*. A number of recent news stories have illustrated that perpetrators of domestic violence may be willing to include anyone in the area in their circle of violence. Think carefully before you involve yourself in domestic violence, and be cautious about *how* you involve yourself if you choose to proceed.

Third, who is involved? It can help to understand the situation to know who is involved. In one disaster in a small and tight-knit community, local providers had reached out to those involved in a particularly difficult accident that had resulted in horrible burns to a number of the town's residents. Those directly affected, family members, and first responders had all received rapid psychological support. But no one had thought about the emergency room staff. Even though it was a very small hospital and despite knowing the injured, the staff had performed spectacularly well with numerous horrendous injuries. In consulting with the psychological support providers, I just asked them to list everyone who had been involved. As they did so, they had the sudden realization that they had overlooked the hospital personnel. That was quickly rectified. Making a list doesn't just ensure that everyone is served, it also can help you to understand the event for which you are providing support.

What has the person already tried? Before you begin to consider possible strategies for solving the problem, it is important to make certain that you understand what the individual has already tried. As you practice active listening, this may be one topic about which to ask questions. Suggesting solutions that the individual has already tried without success can reduce your credibility in providing support. So do not be in too much of a hurry to develop solutions. Stop and make sure you understand the situation.

What strengths does the person have? When beginning to provide support to someone who has a particular problem, it is profitable to do more than just focus on the challenges the problem presents. It is also important to assess what strengths the person brings to the table, and on which the individual may be able to build a solution to the problem. Look at strengths, not just deficits as you assess the situation.

What resources/support system/safety net does the person have? Just as you want to understand the person's own strengths, it is profitable to know what external resources may be available to the individual. These resources include things the person you are supporting may know about. But these resources may also include external programs, nongovernmental organizations (NGO's, also referred to as nonprofit organizations), and agencies of local, state, and federal governments. PFA is not just for terrible events, but for day-to-day problems. Therefore, it is a good idea to learn about what resources there may be in your community on a day-to-day basis. For example, in my home community there is a group similar to Goodwill, which provides clothing and household goods very inexpensively, there are food kitchens, there are churches which own apartments or houses which they use to provide temporary housing to those in need, there are multiple mental health clinics that use a sliding scale (ie, charges are based on income), etc. If a disaster strikes your community, it is likely that there will be additional resources brought to bear by NGO's and government agencies. Try to learn about the benefits of such resources for those whom you will be supporting.

STOP—Build the Relationship

Helping someone develop a problem-solving strategy is easier if you have a good relationship with the person you are supporting. The *BESTT EARS* active listening process, which is described in Chapter 6, is a powerful way to build or maintain a good relationship with the person whom you are supporting. The problem-solving process does not usually begin until after the person whom you are supporting has had the chance to tell you her/his story in the active listening process, so relationship building will have already been taking place before you get to the problem-solving process. Part of active listening, and of being a helper, is unconditional positive regard, discussed in Chapter 6. Showing respect to the individual being supported definitely contributes to the relationship.

Another aspect of building the relationship is to make sure that you do not begin the problem-solving process before the person you are supporting is ready for this step. Dr David Elkind, a developmental psychologist, says that it is important to meet a child where he or she is and draw them forward. Similarly, when you are trying to help someone solve a problem, it is important to make certain that the person you are supporting is ready for that step. If the individual is still trying to understand what has happened to them, it is not yet time to start problem-solving.

The relationship between you as the helper and the person you are supporting is also well-served by maintaining a non-judgmental attitude, something that is also emphasized in active listening. Earlier, in discussing awareness of your own stress, I described the importance of staying calm yourself. That is also helpful in building the relationship with the person whom you are supporting.

The final recommendation in building the relationship is to give the person a sense of hope that things can, indeed, get better. That is a fairly safe assurance. When things are at their worst, they almost always get better. This phenomenon is known as "regression to the mean." Sometimes, when people experience overwhelming events, they can begin to feel that there is no way to make things better. To engage someone in problem-solving, that person needs to believe that solving the problem is possible.

It is important, however, to keep any assurances realistic. I was asked some years ago to review a brochure designed to help parents care for their children after traumatic events. Among the suggestions was that a parent tell his or her child that, "I am in charge now, and nothing more can happen." Now *that* is an unrealistic assurance. No one can control things completely. And if something further does happen (eg, a second tornado striking the same town, thunderstorms following a hurricane, or an earthquake aftershock), the child's trust can be rocked rather severely. So keep your assurances within realistic limits.

STOP—Understand the Person's Feelings and Concerns

Early in this discussion of the *STOP* portion of the *SODA* acronym for problem-solving, I talked about the importance of being aware of your own stress before rushing in to support someone. It is also important to make sure that through your active-listening skills you have gained an understanding of the emotions and concerns of the person you are supporting. This will help you to work with him/her in developing solutions to the problem that fit most effectively in a personal and timely way.

If you feel you do not have that picture adequately yet, follow up with more questions about thoughts and feelings and with overall additional active listening. Active listening is not something you do once and then put away. The active listening continues as you provide CBPFA. Remember that in active listening one of the verbal skills is asking the person what they were thinking or feeling as the event was taking place (eg, "That sounds very difficult. How were you feeling?" or "What were you thinking as that was taking place?"). This can help people understand what they have experienced, and their reactions to it. Remember the *BESTT EARS* active listening acronym. If the person you are supporting begins to feel uncomfortable or that you are prying, explain why you asked the questions. If they are uncomfortable divulging more information to you, proceed as best you can with what you have. It is important not to disrupt your relationship.

STOP—Define/Identify the Main Problem

In many models of problem-solving, clearly identifying the problem to be solved is described as perhaps the hardest part of problem-solving. As was the case for some of the earlier points, this one is inextricably linked with good active listening.

During the active listening, ask the person whom you are supporting what happened. If you ask follow-up questions, try to ask open-ended questions. Open-ended questions cannot be answered with a "yes" or a "no." For example, "Were you scared?" is a closed question. It may give you a single piece of information, but it will not encourage someone to tell you more. However, if you ask an open-ended question such as, "What were you feeling while that was going on?" you are likely to learn whether the person was scared, as well as additional information.

Once you have asked an open-ended question, let the person tell you the story in his/her own way. The goal of this process is to determine what the person whom you are supporting thinks is the problem, to see the problem through her/his eyes. So use the *BESTT EARS* active listening to help you see the challenges from his/her perspective. Part of that process is to make sure that you understand how the problem started, and what the person has done so far to cope.

Options

The entire first portion of the *SODA* problem-solving acronym, *Stop*, is trying to ensure that you are ready to begin the problem-solving process. But once you have prepared with the many steps described previously for the *Stop* portion, and if you think that you clearly understand the problem, it is time to begin to explore options for responding to the problem.

Sometimes you get by with a little help from your friends. Photographer: Euodia Chua.

One way to begin developing a list of options is to ask the person whom you are supporting what strategies have worked for them in the past. This is true even if the current problem is different from anything the person has experienced before.

For a number of years, I studied the prevention of pregnancy and birth complications. I worked with women pregnant for the first time, the group that has the largest number of problems during pregnancy. As I helped some of the women deal with problems they encountered, I asked them what they had done to cope with problems in the past. They usually said that was not relevant, because pregnancy was unlike anything they had experienced before. But learning past successful problem-solving strategies can help to understand what types of problem-solving may be most acceptable to them in the future.

It may also be useful to work together to develop a list of all the possible solutions. It is not profitable during such an exercise to judge the options being listed. Such judgments may inhibit the flow of ideas. There will be plenty of time in the following problem-solving step to reject unlikely solutions.

As mentioned previously, it is important to help the person you are supporting to see the possibility that things can get better. It can be overwhelming when things go badly, and it is not uncommon for people to begin to wonder whether the situation is hopeless. When someone feels that the situation is hopeless, the individual may stop trying to recover. This can be a condition that is very difficult to help the person change.

Decide

Once you have developed a list of options together with the person you are supporting, it is important to select one to put into effect. I generally recommend that the provider and the person receiving the support work together in this process, considering the advantages and disadvantages of each option. I have had many clients over the years who have felt that this strategy was simplistic. But once they have performed the exercise, they have without exception confessed the merits of the technique.

One woman had come into therapy to seek help in making a particularly difficult decision. She had two options and I asked her to write down the benefits and drawbacks to each. When she completed the step, the list of advantages for one was quite long and had few disadvantages, and the lengths of the lists for the other option were just the opposite. She said that it seemed obvious that she had already made the decision.

It is not simply a matter of how long the lists are, however. The content of the advantages and disadvantages is also very important. I think of this every time I hear a television commercial for some prescription medication. So many of them seem to describe a long list of advantages, for example, curing upset stomach. For some of them the list of unwanted side effects is somewhat shorter. But it is frightening how many of those side effects include death. That is a pretty significant side effect, and for myself, at least, outweighs many of the advantages of such medications.

Once you have developed an idea of the benefits and drawbacks of each of your options, it is time to choose which option to put into effect. If you are helping someone else, it is critical that he/she is the once who makes the choice. Try not to rush to a decision. Take the time to make a good choice about how to proceed.

Act

This is the simplest step of all to describe, but perhaps the most difficult to actually carry out. Once you have decided on a course of action, put it into effect. That takes some energy and sometimes courage as well.

Evaluate

Throughout my career I have been frequently surprised at how often people go through the entire problem-solving strategy, put a chosen solution into effect, and stop. I have had clients come to me and complain that they did not understand why they were still experiencing distress, because they had solved the problem. I asked if they had evaluated their solution to see if it truly solved the problem, and they replied that they had not.

It is not enough to choose a solution and enact it. It is necessary to determine whether it worked. If you discover that your solution worked, bravo. If the solution did not accomplish what you had hoped, then go back to the options stage, and work through the problem-solving process again. I think that proponents of this model would say, "Get another *SODA*."

Acceptable Responses

In mainstream US culture, we often limit ourselves to solutions that fix the problem. But one of the things that I encourage people to do in thinking about problem-solving is to consider that there are three types of responses, any one of which may be the best in a specific situation: change the situation; avoid the situation; or tolerate the situation.

Most people who encounter a problem, in my experience, feel that it is best to change the situation and eliminate the problem. But there are times when it may be best to avoid the problem. I have had people tell me on a number of occasions that avoiding the problem was simply cowardice, and should not be tolerated. I think that is a precipitous rush to judgment. I asked one such client, "If there were two routes to your workplace, and one had very heavy traffic and dangerous intersections, whereas the other was an easy and uncrowded drive, would it be cowardly to take the easier route?" He replied that it would, and that he would take the more difficult route! I told him I thought that was an unfortunate choice, but was his to make.

I had another client who was employed in a chemical factory that made explosive materials. He had survived a workplace explosion and was trying to compose himself so that he could return to work. The position he held paid exceptionally well for his level of education, but his workplace had the unfortunate characteristic that it sometimes exploded. After months of therapy, he told me that he had decided to leave the industry for a career that paid much less, but had a much better chance of returning home safely to his family each night. His solution was avoidance, but I think that for him it was a good choice.

Tolerating the situation is often seen as even more unacceptable than avoiding the situation. But it may be the best strategy in some situations. I had a client who came to me to ask me to help him decide how to handle a problem he was having in his workplace. He was only 6 months from becoming eligible for retirement. He had moved up through the company and reached an executive position. His CEO had begun to assign him to very menial and clearly inappropriate tasks, given his position. The client seemed pretty certain that the CEO was trying to get him to leave the corporation, but for various reasons could not outright fire him. We developed a list of options, and considered the benefits and drawbacks of each. In the end, he decided his best course of action was to tolerate the situation. He felt that he could tolerate anything for the 6 months until his retirement. To me that seemed like a perfectly reasonable decision. So if you have a problem, get a *SODA*, and when you look at *Options*, consider the full range of possibilities.

TRY THIS

Start small. If you have children, start out by helping them "get a *SODA.*" Choose a small problem and help them work through it using the *SODA* model. If you do not have children, try working through a problem with another family member, friend, or colleague. Be upfront that you are trying a new strategy, and see what you can accomplish together.

Reference

LaFromboise, T. D. (1996). *American Indian life skills development curriculum.* Madison: University of Wisconsin Press.

8

COPING WITH STRESS

Basic Coping Strategies

Armed with a good understanding of stress and traumatic stress, how can one learn to cope with the stress one experiences? I often tell my students that, "Mom was right!" In training I have conducted all over the world, I ask participants how their parents suggested that they cope with stressful events in their lives as they were growing up. Certainly parents' knowledge about good coping skills varies, but it is amazing to me how many times people quickly list a series of empirically proven strategies for coping with the stressful events of life. So, you may already know a lot of good strategies for coping with stress. But a reminder of these common-sense strategies can be useful. As you read through these basic concepts of self-care, see how many of these proven techniques you already knew (and how many you once knew, but had forgotten, or at least no longer think about). It may also be useful to keep this chapter handy for yourself, because as much as these strategies may seem like common sense, remember that in the midst of traumatic stress one may not remember or appreciate the need for these coping techniques.

Community-Based Psychological First Aid. http://dx.doi.org/10.1016/B978-0-12-804292-2.00008-9

CASE EXAMPLE

A psychologist was approached by a representative of a large nursing school nationally known as being one of the most difficult nursing programs in the country. The administrator told the psychologist that the nursing school had a very high dropout rate and that the administration wanted to give the students more tools to manage the stress of the rigorous academic program. The school's administration had heard that the psychologist taught a form of relaxation including progressive muscle relaxation, word-association techniques, and the use of cognitive imagery and that the classes had become very popular. They asked the psychologist to teach an optional relaxation class for the nursing students to try to help them manage their stress and hopefully result in fewer students dropping out. The school arranged for an informational meeting to talk with interested students about the idea. More than a third of all the students attended. The cost of the training was low, but many of the young college students were already budgeting every penny. One of the students asked what was involved, and the psychologist explained that there would be four weekly sessions in which the next set of skills would be taught. In between those sessions, students would be asked to spend 20–30 min each day practicing that week's techniques. This produced cries of despair and even laughter in the room. A number of the students cried out that they did not have enough time to study as it was, much less to add another 20–30 min to their day. The psychologist responded, encouraging them to try it, explaining that excessive stress levels made it harder to study effectively. The psychologist further predicted that if they would learn the relaxation techniques and practice daily, they would actually have more time to study and learn than they did then, because stress interfered with good cognitive processing. The students were offered a money back guarantee if they did not have that experience. The psychologist was quite pleasantly surprised that a large number of the students signed up for the training, and there had to be several different groups taught. Although skeptical at first, the students soon became enthusiastic about the training. Not a single student asked for a refund of the course registration fee.

Getting Adequate Sleep

One of the most important strategies for managing stress is to do one's best to get adequate sleep. The national news has reported several studies in recent months that continue to indicate that most people do not get enough sleep. The adult human body seems to genuinely need about 8 hours of sleep every night to function at peak levels. Younger people need even more. Getting adequate sleep after experiencing a traumatic event can definitely be challenging, but the additional physical and psychological fatigue in coping with the aftermath of an event may well help one get to sleep if the body is just given a chance to stop (stop moving, stop watching television, stop emailing, stop texting/tweeting/etc.) for a while. It is profitable to try to follow one's usual routines in getting ready for bed. Further, try to get horizontal and consciously make an effort to relax the legs, abdomen, chest, arms, neck, and head. Then, think about something other than the traumatic event or how one is going to recover from it. Try to concentrate on a calm scene, the calmest place one can imagine. Make it as real in the mind as possible, adding visual detail, even imagining the sounds and smells. The brain will often do the rest.

Getting adequate sleep is very important, both physically and psychologically. This is true despite the possibility of nightmares and the possible extra time that may be needed to get to sleep.

Eating Well

It is very useful to make the effort to eat well-balanced meals, and avoid too much sugar, fats, caffeine, and alcohol. This is a key component of an effective coping strategy. Eating well-balanced meals, even when someone does not feel hungry is important to maintaining health and effectiveness. The body needs good nutrition even when we do not feel like eating. Good nutrition not only helps the body but also increases the ability to cope psychologically with the stress of the event.

Similarly, many people turn to caffeine when they feel stressed, believing that it sharpens their thinking and alertness. A little caffeine may be fine, but a lot of caffeine causes problems and can greatly reduce one's ability to function at peak performance. About 30 years ago, I knew a graduate student who loved good coffee and had recently acquired a new appliance for his office, an espresso machine. Specialty coffee shops were not as common then. He had read that espresso was very high-quality coffee, and had decided to indulge himself by buying the machine. He loved good coffee and felt that the caffeine helped him manage the stress of the very demanding graduate program. A few days after he got the new machine working, he came to talk to me informally. He was not one of my students, but his office was close to mine. He said he was a bit concerned that he might be developing a neurological disorder because he had developed a significant tremor in his hands, and knowing that I had worked in neuropsychology, he asked what I thought. I looked at his hands, which were visibly shaking, and asked him how many cups of espresso he was drinking. He said the cups were so small that he had about 16 cups a day since the machine arrived… or may be a few more than that. Too much of even a good thing may cause problems.

CASE EXAMPLE

In one mass casualty event those working in the recovery of human remains were mostly law-enforcement professionals. The incident manager, who oversees the entire response operation, knew that too much caffeine could make it harder to manage stress. Therefore he had ordered that there be no caffeine available at the isolated location where the recovery efforts were taking place. The supervisor overseeing the provision of food and drink to the officers approached the disaster mental health manager and frantically asked that the psychologist please talk with the incident commander because the officers involved in the recovery were *very* angry about the lack of caffeine and were demanding in the strongest terms that the food services produce regular coffee. He concluded his high-pitched appeal with, "… and those guys carry guns!" The psychologist approached the incident commander and applauded him for thinking about limiting caffeine, but pointed out that caffeine is actually an addictive drug, and that the middle of a recovery effort was not a good time to have the entire crew of law-enforcement officers going through withdrawal. The incident commander understood and ordered that caffeine be allowed, but that the officers be encouraged to limit their intake. Things quickly calmed down.

Sometimes instead of eating a balanced nutritious diet there is a temptation when stress levels rise to turn to "comfort food." This term refers to food that feels like an indulgence, and is usually food that stimulates happy childhood memories. It is often food that is high in sugar and/or fat. A certain amount of such indulgence is fine, but overdoing it increases one's difficulty in managing stress both physically and psychologically.

Exercise

Exercise can be useful even if it was not part of one's routine before the disaster. Physical exertion, appropriate to one's age and physical condition, can help to reduce both physical and psychological tension, and can be a very valuable tool in the aftermath of disaster. Moreover, getting fit before one experiences a traumatic event can help the individual manage the stress. You may recall that in Spielberger's model of individual reactions to stress (Chapter 3), one of the factors that directly affects cognitive appraisal is the physical state of the individual. Better physical condition is likely to mean less perception of stress than one would otherwise have.

TRY THIS

The basic coping strategies described previously can improve your life even when you are not experiencing difficult times. Consider how you can do better at each of the three.

Getting Adequate Sleep

Try deliberately scheduling your day so that you can actually get 8 hours of sleep every night. That may mean cutting out a late-night talk show, or turning off the computer, tablet, or cell phone a little earlier, but the payoff both in terms of health and ability to cope with stress will be a tangible reward.

Eating Well

I am not suggesting that you become a health-food fanatic. Small changes can have significant benefits. Make a list of all the foods you eat in a day. Try making a commitment to cut out one source of fat and one source of sugar, or cut the serving size for those foods in half. Is the portion of meat that you eat double the recommended serving size? Try reducing the excess by half. Are you eating less than the recommended portion of fruits and vegetables? Try increasing the amount by half for at least one meal a day.

Exercise

If you can afford to, try getting one of the many popular activity monitors. If an activity monitor does not fit your budget, try to keep track of the number of minutes you are walking or the number of stairs you climb in a day. Check your existing activity levels and then set realistic moderate goals to increase your activity levels. Try small changes such as parking farther away from your destination instead of taking the closest parking place. Walk one flight up or two flights down rather than taking the elevator. Use the rest room two floors up and take the stairs rather than using the rest room on your same floor. Small changes can make a big difference.

Coping After a Traumatic Event

Taking Breaks

It is important for people to take a measured approach to managing their recovery from a traumatic event. Sometimes people feel that any time they take for themselves after a disaster is time that is wasted, and that taking time for oneself may actually be wrong or "sinful." It is common in the aftermath of events to see many people pushing themselves until they drop, whether in recovering their own affairs or in helping others. The problem with this strategy is that the ability to be effective steadily declines with prolonged continuous work hours, and the effort expended becomes steadily less useful, until a person's efforts may even be counterproductive and actually interfere with effective recovery. In addition, this constant driven behavior may result in dangerous levels of physical and psychological stress on the individual.

Taking breaks is critically important in self-care. Photographer: Euodia Chua.

CASE EXAMPLE

During one mass casualty incident one mental health professional refused to leave at the end of his shift at the facility where the survivors and families were housed. The manager in charge of mental health for the disaster-relief operation spoke with the volunteer, but the man refused to leave. The manager decided that forcing the man out might cause a scene and might reflect badly on the man, and allowed him to stay, but asked one of the other mental health workers to watch him carefully. As the number of hours the man had been working increased, as well as the number of hours since he had last had sleep, he became less effective. He still refused to leave, so the manager changed his assignment to office tasks that did not involve contact with the survivors or families. The man's usefulness steadily declined. Still refusing to go off-duty, the manager assigned him to walk about the facility, counting how many people were in each of the public rooms. The worker found this quite reasonable, and duly walked about, carefully counting for several hours, before falling asleep in a chair in the disaster mental health office. He slept for many hours, oblivious to all the activity going on about him.

When he woke up, he went and found the manager (who had returned after a solid night's sleep) and apologized. He said that after having slept for many hours, he fully understood how inappropriate his refusal had been, and although he could not remember everything he had done during the interim, he realized that he had been very ineffective and he was extremely embarrassed. He told the manager that he understood that his actions had been unprofessional, that he was going home to take a more formal rest, and that he planned to continue to work in disaster mental health, but would never again stay beyond the end of his shift.

During the response to the crash of Flight 232, the aviation disaster that was in many ways the beginning of our Disaster Mental Health Institute, a national figure in disaster response approached me and said, "Your doctoral students are total professionals." I thanked him and agreed, but asked him what had led him to make the comment. To my surprise, he replied that the evidence of their professionalism was that they knew when to take a break, knew when to say "No" to a request to take on additional work when they were already fully occupied, refused assignments that were beyond their skill levels, left at the end of their scheduled shift, and that they had gotten some sleep before returning to the operation for their next shift. Rather than the quality of their interventions and their knowledge of crisis intervention, his favorable impression was dominated by the doctoral students' skills at self-care. All of us in disaster response know that self-care is critical to remaining effective in the lengthy process of recovery from a traumatic event.

Taking breaks during the day and trying to focus for a few minutes on something other than the traumatic event is very important. Talk with someone about something other than the present situation. Play a game. Read something. Check your Facebook. These breaks can be very renewing and enable the person to be far more effective for a far longer time. Working fewer hours and at a measured pace will probably help someone get more done than working continuously until exhausted.

Maintain a Routine

It is useful for individuals to maintain a routine similar to their pre-event routine. The familiar is comforting, especially for children. Maintain a familiar routine to the extent possible after an event. This may be challenging for those sleeping in shelters or simply because of the chaos that can exist after an event. But to the extent possible, reestablish nighttime rituals and habits such as cleaning up and brushing teeth before bed.

Trying to have meals at regular times, reinstituting morning rituals and other routines can also be very useful. The disaster relief workers who focus on feeding survivors work very hard to provide meals at the same time every day, giving survivors something they can depend on, something predictable in the midst of chaos.

Even sitting down and doing homework when a child gets back from school can be comforting for a child if this was the child's routine before the event. Similarly, if someone usually took an evening walk before bed, or exercised at some point during the day, restoring that routine can decrease the stress of the aftermath of an event.

Avoid Excessive "Self-Medication"

Sometimes individuals may turn to using excessive amounts of alcohol or other drugs in an effort to self-medicate and escape the stress of the event. The problem is that this strategy is very temporary and may increase the magnitude of problems with which the individual needs to cope. Using substances to avoid stress reactions has the effect of simply delaying having to cope with the experience. In addition, the use of alcohol and some other substances may lead to an increased risk of family violence, which can severely aggravate the recovery of an entire family after an event. An intoxicated individual is certainly unlikely to be able to provide the psychological support that children need in a normal situation, much less when children are trying to manage unusually high levels of stress.

Support From and For Family and Friends

Most individuals receive the great majority of their psychological support from family and friends. With this knowledge, it is important for individuals to take time to be with their families and friends, both for their own enjoyment as well as to both provide and receive psychological support. It is important for individuals to both talk with and listen to family and friends about their experiences and feelings. So taking the time to be together can be a rich opportunity for healing for oneself, as well as a gift to one's family and friends. It may be useful to remember that if family and friends do not provide all the psychological support needed, it may be necessary for individuals to turn to elders, religious advisors, primary care (medical) providers, or even mental health professionals.

Giving and receiving psychological support with family and friends is an important part of coping. Photographer: Euodia Chua.

Overcoming Challenges to Coping

These self-care principles may seem simple on paper and when reading them in the midst of a routine day, with no more than usual levels of stress. But it is much more challenging to re-member, much less to practice, these strategies in the midst of chaos. Traumatic stress reactions can make cognitive processing less effective. It is difficult to do even simple things while coping with extreme stress. So, as strange as it may seem as you read this, it may be necessary to remind individuals that these common-sense strategies remain useful and may be even more important in the aftermath of a traumatic event.

Participating in Recovery Efforts Can Be Healing

We know that people who withdraw from family, friends, and colleagues have more difficulty in recovering from traumatic stress. This is primarily true if that behavior is different from the person's behavior before the event. But there is evidence that iso-lation itself, regardless of whether it was the person's style before the event, puts people at risk. One way to prevent isolation is to get involved in the recovery effort, whether that means starting to pick up the pieces of one's own life, or helping friends and neighbors pick up what remains of theirs.

Alfred Adler (Alfie) was a contemporary of Sigmund Freud (Ziggy). Alfie does not get as much ink as Ziggie in our modern society. But in the early 20th century, when these two giants of psychological theory were developing their theories in Austria, Alfie may have been the more popular of the two figures among the general population in their home city of Vienna. Ziggie worked primarily with wealthy members of high society, focusing on their sex lives and generally causing scandal in the society as the result of his sexually oriented theories. Alfie focused more on everyday people and their real day-to-day problems. One of his most common therapeutic interventions was to have his patients go out during the week between sessions and serve the poor. He would have them work in soup kitchens or work as assistants in medical clinics for the poor. He believed that serving others in need was one of the most powerful ways to improve one's own life. This was a powerful concept at the time, but was displaced in time by the titillation and excitement of Freud's open discussion of sex lives at a time when such matters were not mentioned in polite company. Freud became the father of psychotherapy, and Adler was reduced nearly to a footnote. But time and science have suggested that Adler had great insight and may have been more on-target than Freud.

A Word of Caution

Although it is profitable to be involved in recovery efforts, it is important to do so in measured ways. In the immediate aftermath of terrible events lives may hang in the balance. People may be alive and trapped in rubble due to earthquakes, tornados, hurricanes, or other destructive events. It is understandable that people may work intensely during the immediate postimpact phase of the disaster, searching for the missing. When lives are in danger, making the decision to work for a period of time without breaks is reasonable. It is possible to do that effectively for a while. But even in those circumstances it is important to monitor one's own condition to make sure one is not endangering oneself or others who might be impacted if fatigue reduces one's effectiveness and judgment. If lives are going to be in danger for days at a time, or if lives are not in danger, it is very advantageous to practice good self-care. In doing so, one's efforts in the recovery will be more effective, and good self-regulation will provide a degree of protection to oneself and to one's family, and, perhaps, to those around the individual.

9

PROVIDING INSTRUMENTAL (PRACTICAL) ASSISTANCE

When your active listening has begun to give you a picture of the experiences of the person for whom you are providing support, it may be appropriate to offer some instrumental or practical assistance. Your active listening (*BESTT EARS*) will probably give you a good sense of what needs the person has, and whether some simple practical help could ease their burden or lift their spirits. Instrumental assistance simply means that you support the individual in doing some of the practical things that need to be done next in the situation, or by providing some physical assistance.

At the crash of Flight 232 as our team provided support to the survivors on the night of the crash I was very pleased to see that my doctoral students were providing the families with whom they

Community-Based Psychological First Aid. http://dx.doi.org/10.1016/B978-0-12-804292-2.00009-0

were working with blankets, pillows, food, and drinks. They knew from their training that people who are physically comfortable are also more psychologically comfortable. Over my decades in disaster psychology, I have seen a number of mental health professionals who felt that instrumental assistance was beneath their dignity as a professional. But most know that simple instrumental assistance can be very comforting and soothing for someone who has experienced a traumatic event.

The ideas described subsequently are by no means a comprehensive description of all that can be done to provide instrumental assistance. Many of the things that can be done to provide instrumental assistance are common sense. I challenged the undergraduate students in one of my classes to list the things that might be able to be done to provide instrumental assistance for someone who had experienced a disaster. In a short time just using their common sense they generated a list that included many of these ideas. Again, it is important to realize that although this information may seem simplistic, in the midst of overwhelming stress, many common-sense strategies may be hard to remember. You can probably think of many more, particularly when you are working with someone who has told you about their experiences and needs through your active listening.

Preparation

In the field of disaster relief, professionals learn that much of the work in disaster response is best done before a disaster ever occurs. Disaster preparedness makes the work in the moment of the disaster and in the aftermath tremendously easier. The same can be true in providing instrumental assistance in CBPFA. One strategy that I would strongly encourage you to adopt is to complete first aid and CPR (cardiopulmonary resuscitation) training, which are available through many community organizations, perhaps most notably through the American Red Cross and the American Heart Association.

For Your Own Home

With regard to your own family and your own home, it is profitable to know how to turn off the gas, electricity, and water for your home. Your utility company(ies) can provide that information if none of your family members knows. Realize too, that after gas has been turned off, there are safety procedures to follow before the gas is turned back on, because pilot lights will have gone out if the gas has been off.

TRY THIS

Take the time now to investigate resources in your community.

American Red Cross chapter
Location:_____
Phone:_____

Salvation Army
Location:_____
Phone:_____

Goodwill Store
Location:_____
Phone:_____

Second-Hand Clothing
Name of Facility #1_____
Location:_____
Phone:_____

Name of Facility #2_____
Location:_____
Phone:_____

Soup Kitchen/Food Pantry
Name of Facility #1_____
Location:_____
Phone:_____

Name of Facility #2_____
Location:_____
Phone:_____

Food Stamp Office
Location:_____
Phone:_____

Temporary Housing
Location:_____
Phone:_____

Other Resources
Name of Facility #1_____
Location:_____
Phone:_____

Name of Facility #2_____
Location:_____
Phone:_____

Name of Facility #3_____
Location:_____
Phone:_____

Educate Yourself About Resources in Your Neighborhood/Town/City

In order to provide effective instrumental support it is useful to know what agencies, services, or charitable organizations may be available to provide assistance to individuals or families on a daily basis as well as in the aftermath of a disaster. Many of the organizations that contribute to disaster response (eg, American Red Cross, Salvation Army) are permanent parts of their communities. Other agencies may offer assistance to affected communities only in the aftermath of a disaster (eg, FEMA).

Does your city have an American Red Cross chapter? A Salvation Army store? A Goodwill store? A second-hand clothing store? A soup kitchen or food pantry? Are there faith-based organizations that provide some of these same services, or provide other similar services? For example, Faith-in Action is a national faith-based organization that matches people in need with volunteers who can help them, providing rides to medical appointments, home repairs, etc. There are also civic organizations that provide home repairs, second-hand clothing, furniture, and appliances. Some faith-based groups provide temporary housing for those in need.

There may also be government offices in the area in which you live that offer services relevant in daily life as well as in the aftermath of disaster. Government offices may provide temporary housing or food stamps. County agricultural extension agents may have information regarding recovery from disasters (eg, how to clean items soiled by flood waters). Some school districts or public libraries have lending "libraries" that include children's toys and books, board games, and video games which may be able to fill the gap in children's entertainment as a family works on recovery from a disaster.

After Traumatic Events: Emergency Phase

Update Information About Resources in Your Area

After a disaster occurs it is useful to update your knowledge of resources available in your area to ensure that you have as much information as may be useful to those whom you are supporting. This is a form of preparedness that takes place after the event to add to the knowledge you developed before the event. Try to find out which resources you learned about before the disaster are still operating after the event.

Further, try to learn what additional agencies may have come to provide disaster relief and where they are located. Where have insurance companies set up their offices? If cell phone towers and telephone land lines were affected, are there any banks of telephones that have been set up for affected families to use? Some companies even bring in mobile laundromats which they make available without charge to disaster-affected individuals. Nondisaster related resources are also important. Are any gasoline stations operating? What churches are still functioning? What groceries and pharmacies are still available? What schools may be opening and when?

First Steps After the Event

If you are providing support to someone soon after a disaster, it may be useful to determine whether a few initial safety steps have been taken. It is important to determine whether the person you are serving is in need of physical first aid. I have seen individuals in some disasters working enthusiastically in the immediate aftermath of a disaster despite having fairly significant injuries. Adrenaline can mask pain and injury, but immediate attention to injuries such as broken bones, wounds, and burns can prevent more serious consequences later. Depending on the person's pre-event medical condition, it may be important to make sure the person has medications that are critical to them. Both of these needs can be met by the American Red Cross disaster relief operation.

If the home of the person whom you are supporting has been affected, it may be useful to help the person think about whether it is safe to return to the home. Few of us are qualified to determine the structural integrity of a house. Government building inspectors will most commonly have that role. If you have any concerns whatsoever, it is profitable to let the professionals make such determinations and help the person or family whom you are supporting find temporary housing.

CASE EXAMPLE

Hurricane Andrew in 1992 had some of the strongest winds recorded in a hurricane. One network news anchor did a live broadcast in front of a house in the heart of the destruction. He pointed out the home behind him and said that it was remarkable that there were homes that were virtually undamaged, despite the enormous destruction all around. I happened to know that the house he was pointing out was actually assessed as totally destroyed. Some of the homes looked fine at first glance, other than broken windows and a few missing shingles. But the extreme winds, entering the houses through the broken windows, had inflated the houses like balloons, pushing the walls out and leaving houses quite unstable and dangerous. In one tornado disaster to which I responded I was responsible for damage assessment. One of the homes there was similarly affected. Viewed casually, the home seemed fine. But if you looked carefully at the walls, you could see that all of them were slanting out from the center of the house and the building was in imminent danger of collapse. Similarly, earthquakes and floods can cause relatively subtle damage that can severely impact the integrity of a building. Be cautious about entering affected buildings.

Be very cautious and do not go beyond your own knowledge and comfort level. Following a flood or storm surge, for example, checking if the electricity is on in the house can be very dangerous. It would probably be best to check with a knowledgeable authority for some guidance before you begin. Utility companies and county agricultural extension offices may be able to help in this regard.

If those whom you are supporting insist on staying in or going back into their home, it is profitable to consider a few other steps to increase the safety of the home. Perhaps the next highest priority is to help the person whom you are supporting make sure the gas is turned off if the gas lines may have been affected (eg, following an earthquake). Further, help the client assess the livability of the house by checking to see if water is running, if there is electricity, and whether the refrigerator, stove, or other necessary appliances are working. If you are in a cold climate, check to see if the heating system is working.

Again, however, it is profitable to call in professionals or a representative of the utility company.

Less Urgent Concerns: Communicating with Family

Communicating with family may not be as immediate a need as the safety of the person whom you are supporting and of the person's house. For many individuals, however, communicating with family members is very important in coping with the aftermath of an event. Researchers have learned that individuals who are separated from their families during a disaster are far more likely to have difficulty coping with the event. The more quickly one can get in touch with missing family members, the quicker one is likely to recover.

This step may be as simple as helping the individual place a phone call to let family members know they have survived a disaster. It is most useful to have individuals do it themselves, but they may need some assistance. You might at first think, "How can someone need help making a phone call?" But remember that traumatic stress often interferes with cognitive functioning. After a traumatic event, previously simple tasks may suddenly seem overwhelming. As noted previously, it may be necessary to find a local temporary phone bank to use if local land lines and cell towers have been destroyed.

Other strategies for reuniting family members who lived in the affected area or communicating with family outside the affected area may involve contacting the American Red Cross Family Welfare Activity. These disaster-relief workers coordinate with federal authorities and with Red Cross chapters across the country and around the world in trying to locate and reunite separated families, and communicate with distant family members (when asked). The American Red Cross provides an online service called Safe and Well that can also help family and friends communicate.

Less Urgent Concerns: Food

It may be helpful to assist the person you are supporting in determining what food the individual or family will need in the subsequent few days. Helping fulfill those needs may be as simple as helping make a shopping list. Hopefully in your postdisaster preparedness you learned whether grocery stores were open. What foods may be best in the current circumstances? Is refrigeration a possibility? Is there a means of heating or cooking food? Is there a means of getting to the store, and practically getting groceries back home? The American Red Cross Disaster Relief Operation may be providing funds for emergency food purchases. If obtaining groceries is not practical, what other sources of food may be available? Are the American Red Cross or the Salvation Army providing feeding services at a shelter or feeding site? Are local food banks or soup kitchens operating?

Less Urgent Concerns: Clothing

In some disasters, survivors may have little more than the clothes they had on their backs when the event occurred. In your preparedness, you hopefully learned where the American Red Cross Disaster Relief Operation is providing services to families, whether there is a Salvation Army facility in the area, and whether there are second-hand clothing stores locally. This information can be very helpful for those to whom you are providing psychological support.

Less Urgent Concerns: Temporary Housing

Your preparedness efforts before and after the event may have revealed what temporary housing options may be available. Depending on the event, the Red Cross may be operating shelters.

As noted earlier, many communities have state offices that provide temporary housing. It is also fairly common for some churches to have houses or apartments that they maintain to provide emergency housing when needed. If those for whom you are providing psychological support have need of temporary housing, a survey of local churches may provide some possibilities.

Helping someone move into replacement housing is an example of instrumental assistance. Photographer: Euodia Chua.

In some disasters, there is little need for shelters because family, friends, and neighbors provide temporary housing. Opening your home to family and neighbors is a significant step to take, so think carefully before you offer to have someone share your home. It is important that your whole family has the opportunity to discuss the implications of sharing their living space with those who have been displaced by the event. The likely reduction in privacy and disruption of family routines may impose significant stress on your own family during a time when there may already be added stress due to the impact of the event on the community. One important factor is to have an idea of how long the need for temporary housing is likely to be. For a short-term event it may be much easier to have houseguests than for an event that may take weeks or months to resolve.

Less Urgent Concerns: Child Care

As families try to recover from a disaster, parents may be significantly occupied with recovery of physical items from their homes, repairing the family's residence, and/or the process of paperwork that is commonly involved in obtaining disaster relief services. (It is becoming more common for disaster assistance applications to be completed online. Unfortunately, in the aftermath of a disaster, electricity, cell phone services, and internet services may be disrupted, resulting in a return to old fashioned paperwork.) Wage earners in the family may need to return to work. Schools and community child care centers may not have reopened. This creates a great need for someone to care for children while the parents complete some of the tasks needed for the family to recover from the event. In large-scale disasters, faith-based national teams sometimes set up professional child care services in collaboration with the American Red Cross disaster relief operation. Particularly if such services are not available, providing some child care or babysitting yourself or organizing some community child care or babysitting exchange can be a significant relief for parents. Furthermore, providing some focused attention and simple, fun activities to allow them to think about something other than the disaster or traumatic event may also be a source of psychological support for the children.

Some readers may be very familiar with the challenges of caring for children. But if you are not, it is important to realize that caring for children can be challenging. Chapter 14 provides an idea of some of the challenges children face after a traumatic event. A great deal of energy, focused attention, and a large stockpile of patience are likely to be needed by a caregiver. Knowledge of developmentally appropriate activities for children is also useful. Many child care professionals have bachelor's degrees and even graduate degrees, representing years of study of children's needs as well as educational strategies to serve those needs. Moreover, there are likely to be state and/or local laws governing anything beyond simple babysitting.

Consider carefully what it may mean to care for children even for a few hours. A lot of movie and television comedies have been produced on the topic of temporary child care, and there is a seed of truth to many of the challenges portrayed in these often absurd portrayals. The National Association for the Education of Young Children has links to many helpful resources concerning helping children who have experienced disasters and other overwhelming events. Try this link: http://www.naeyc.org/content/disasters-and-tragedies.

Less Urgent Concerns: Recreational Items

Families who have been displaced from their homes are often lacking in recreational items for their children. In many cases, toys and sporting goods from the home are unable to be retrieved or are no longer useable. Having some fresh recreational items (sporting goods, games, art materials, read, puzzles, games, equipment, toys, stuffed animals, blankets for young children) available for the children can be a tremendous help in keeping children occupied and interested. I remember in one mass casualty response, the local department of recreation backed a tractor-trailer up to the Family Assistance Center. The truck unfolded like something out of a Transformers movie, and turned into a basketball court on one side, a play area on the other, and a booth on the end where children (and adults) could check out various balls and recreational toys. It was a wonderful resource for children and adults alike.

Recovery Phase after Traumatic Events

Transportation

In the aftermath of many disasters, transportation can be a significant challenge. Cars may be destroyed or disabled, and public transportation is also often affected. There are many things that adults need to do in the recovery process that involve transportation. You may be able to offer help by giving a ride or arranging for one, or by helping organize carpools or shuttles. Be careful, though, not to compromise your safety. Remember that working in teams can be the safest way to proceed.

Cleanup Knowledge

There are a number of other sources of instrumental assistance that you may be able to help organize. There is often a need to learn some new skills in the aftermath of an event. After house fires, for example, it is helpful to know how to get the smell of smoke out of clothing, carpet, furniture, and walls. After floods and other water events (eg, storm surge) it is important to understand how to restore water-damaged goods and homes. There are agencies that assist with public education workshops. County agricultural extension offices can often provide handouts and even instructors for community trainings on such issues.

Borrowing Networks or Lending "Libraries"

Another service that you may be able to help organize is a "borrowing network" or a tool lending "library." In a borrowing network community, members may provide a list of the tools they own and are willing to share. Other members of the community can approach the owners of the tools they need and sign them out to work on their homes. A tool lending library can sometimes be set up with the cooperation of a hardware store or home improvement store. A set of tools is contributed, either by commercial stores or by community residents and can be "checked out" by those needing to repair their homes.

Photo Exchanges

In the past decade it has become common for communities affected by terrible storms and tornadoes to have photograph exchanges. Photos can be scattered in storms and floods and are one of the very personal items that people often fear can never be replaced. In the aftermath of a storm there may be photos laying all about in the debris. The idea of the photo exchange is that people bring whatever photos they have found to a central location. There the photos are laid out on tables and people are able to scan the tables for lost memories of their families and loved ones. In some cases, it may be possible to have experts in photo restoration or digital transfer of photos available as well.

Social Networking

In addition to repair necessities, there are other activities that can help the community to recover. These may include social events, play dates for children, babysitting exchange networks, or clothing and food drives. There are many variations of such traditional activities in different cultures.

Psychological support can include both Active Listening and exercise.
Photographer: Gerard Jacobs.

Basic Coping Skills

Finally, there are some other simple things you can do to provide instrumental assistance. For example, simply encouraging those you are serving to physically exercise can provide good psychological support. This may be as simple as taking a walk while you talk.

Summary

Instrumental assistance is not a necessary part of CBPFA, but it is one additional tool in your toolbox for psychological support. Many providers of CBPFA find themselves wanting to do something more concrete than active listening. Fairly simple instrumental assistance can help both the CBPFA provider and the client feel better. These concrete strategies can be an effective part of problem-solving.

10

LOSS AND GRIEVING

One thing that has been striking to me from my work with those who have been affected by mass casualty events across the United States and in working with individuals who have suffered more individual losses through the death of a loved one, is the degree to which the mainstream American culture tries to avoid the grieving process. People who have experienced the death of a loved one are often chided by friends and family if they do not "move on" within a few days of the death.

In one amazingly poignant incident I remember a mother whose teenage son was killed in a freak accident. One moment the young man was a model member of the small town where his family lived, and the next moment he was dead in an unavoidable event and through absolutely no fault of his own. The family and the entire community were overwhelmed with grief. The entire community participated in the funeral and burial. The day after the funeral the mother's employer called and told her it was time to "get over it" and get back to work.

Many widows have told me that people can be amazingly insensitive and unsupportive of their grieving and recovery. People often criticize them when the widows find themselves overwhelmed by memories of their husbands a few weeks or months after the deaths. People want them to "get closure." I think it is more likely that the people around these grieving widows are actually the ones uncomfortable with the emotions and just want it to go away. It is as if they are saying, "Sure the man who was half of your life for the past 40 years died, but come on. It is already been a month. Get on with life."

Similarly, parents of children who have died have told me of tremendously clumsy attempts by friends and family to be supportive.

Community-Based Psychological First Aid. http://dx.doi.org/10.1016/B978-0-12-804292-2.00010-7

I myself have heard people say to the parents at the funeral home, "Well, at least you have other children" or "Thank heavens you're young and you can have another one." One wonders if people would be able to see how brutal such comments are if they were able to somehow step back from the moment and see it as if in a movie or television show. Would they recognize how harsh such comments feel to the grieving parents?

The process of grieving the death of a loved one can easily take a year or more even for very strong individuals. And it is not a process of "getting closure." You do not suddenly close the door on that former portion of your life and open a door to a new one. Rather, it is a process of adapting to the new life situation without the deceased loved one, to find a "new normal." It is developing new routines for breakfast or dinner or bedtime. People often do not realize how much their routines are intertwined with the routines of loved ones until the loved ones are gone. When the surviving family member goes through all the routines of the day, every time the survivor comes to a moment which would normally involve interacting with the deceased loved one, the survivor is reminded of the loss in their life. Over time that realization becomes less of a virtual slap in the face and more of a dull and painful reminder. Slowly the survivor constructs a "new normal" set of daily routines and adapts to the loss.

TRY THIS

During the next week, try to pay attention to how often your daily routines intertwine with a family member, friend, or colleague. Think about how frequently you would be reminded if one of them died.

People with spiritual beliefs in an afterlife may experience additional stress because of their grief, feeling that they "should" be happy for the loved one, because according to their beliefs the loved one now is in eternal happiness. I would suggest that these folks are expecting too much of themselves. Yes, their loved one may be in unending bliss. But the survivor is still left to construct a new normal life without the daily presence, love, and support of the deceased. And even for persons with strong faith, in whichever religious perspective or worldview, creating a new normal after the death of a loved one is likely to be difficult at times.

What to Say

First of all, I strongly recommend that you do not talk to someone about the death of their loved one unless you know for certain that they have been officially notified that their loved one has died. You do not want the family to think that you are delivering a death notice or that you have written off a missing loved one. If you are working in a situation where people are missing in some kind of an event, begin by asking whether the family has heard anything about the status of their loved one. If they have not heard for sure, stick to talking with them about how they are coping with the situation. Do not push into trying to process grief if the family is not even sure that their loved one has died.

Second, do not be afraid to say something for fear of reminding the person of the deceased loved one. Within at least the first few weeks and probably months, the deceased loved one is unlikely to be out of the survivor's awareness for more than a few moments. The individual is much more likely to be upset if you *do not* acknowledge the death, if you have not already previously done so.

CASE EXAMPLE

I saw a colleague at a grocery store recently. It was the first time I had seen him since his father had died, nearly a month earlier. I approached him and offered my condolences. He expressed his deep appreciation that I had remembered, and we talked for some time about memories of his father.

In one aviation disaster I was asked to be the American Red Cross spokesperson in the first meeting of the families of those on board the aircraft. I spoke after a number of federal, state, and local government representatives, briefed families on procedures and progress in the recovery and the crash investigation in a very efficient and business-like manner. When I took the podium, I said, "First let me begin by offering condolences to all of you on the deaths of your loved ones on behalf of all of the American Red Cross disaster services workers in this operation." The crowd of family members actually cheered, and several shouted comments such as, "It's about time somebody said something." They just wanted to know that we were aware of their grieving and that it made a difference to us. I know for a fact that the government officials there cared as well. I think they avoided saying something simply because they were uncomfortable with the grief themselves.

A bit earlier in the chapter I mentioned the importance of avoiding some unprofitable phrases. One of the classic "no-win" statements is to say, "I know how you feel." Almost 100% of the time, the individual will think, and will often say out loud, "No, you don't."

So what are profitable things to say? I think it is almost always safe to say, "I want to offer my condolences on the death of your loved one." Note that I say "death" and not "loss." People have often told me that they resent it when people dance around the issue. I have heard people offer condolences on the loss of a loved one, to which the family member has replied, "I didn't *lose* anything. My husband died."

CASE EXAMPLE

On one occasion a colleague who had joined our faculty only weeks earlier died in a car accident. I was shocked when the university asked me to speak with the family on behalf of the university. I knew him so little, but had enjoyed beginning to get to know him and I struggled with what to say to them. I found a phrase that has been useful to me many times since then when acquaintances have died. After I offered our department's condolences, I added, "Please know that in some small way, we share your sense of loss."

Perhaps the most important point is that, whatever you say, be truthful. If you attempt to portray emotions or feelings that are fake, the person you are trying to support is likely to know it, and your credibility as a provider could be severely damaged.

Cultural Differences and Rituals

If you are providing psychological support to communities other than your own, be sure you understand the cultural practices and attitudes. There are some cultures in which it is considered rude to mention the death of someone's family member. There are other cultures in which the way one addresses the death is important.

There are also rituals in many cultures to help the family and the community come to grips with a death. Most people in mainstream American culture are familiar with ceremonies at funeral homes, funerals, and burials. These are ritualized events. In different cultures, these same words are used for very different procedures.

CASE EXAMPLE

About 9 months after the December 26, 2004 Asian tsunami I was asked to conduct a training of trainers for psychological support in Sri Lanka, which had suffered extensive devastation and thousands of deaths in the event. As we talked about grieving rituals in the training, one of the participants asked if we could buy a set of flags. I had no idea what he meant, but asked him to tell me about the importance of the flags. In some Buddhist communities (Sri Lanka is about 80% Buddhist) when a family member dies, the village flies a particular color of flags along the streets. The flags are a different color at the home of the family whose loved one has died. This is a public statement by both the community and the family that a loved one has died. In the aftermath of the tsunami, everything had been destroyed and/or washed away. There were no flags to proclaim the deaths that had been suffered. So many had died, but the families and the communities had not been able to acknowledge those deaths in the traditional ways. When I asked about how much a set of flags would cost, they told me a set cost about $2.00. I told them I had no financial authority in the program, but I would buy a set for each village if the program would not. Throughout the southern coast of Sri Lanka where these trainers were working the flags appeared in village after village. Almost every family in the region had family members die in the tsunami, and families took turns flying the colors over their tent, or shed, or their new house that indicated that in their family a loved one had died.

In Lakota tradition it is common for family members to cut their hair when a loved one dies, and it is rude to acknowledge the new haircut. They also may perform a "giveaway" ceremony a year after a loved one's death. This involves giving away things the family owns to neighbors, friends, and even to strangers. The more one gives away, the greater the expression of love for the deceased. I have been told that sometimes the family literally gives away everything they own in an outpouring of their love and in an expression of their grief. The community, in turn, gives back to them the basics they need to start their lives over. It is a powerful expression of the grieving process, a year after the death, and a powerful demonstration of community love and support.

Stages of Grief

Elizabeth Kubler-Ross has written extensively about a model for understanding the resolution of grief following the death of a loved one. There has been a great deal of discussion of her theories in the professional literature over the years. There are much more complex theories now that probably do explain the grieving process more accurately. But I think Kubler-Ross' theory can help us understand some of the things that grieving individuals experience. Basically, she suggested that people go through a series of steps or stages as they progress toward a new normal without the living presence of their loved one. Generally, according to the theory, people begin by denying that their loved one has died. I have frequently seen this occur in aviation disasters, with family members insisting that the body or remains identified by the medical examiner as their loved one was misidentified, that their loved one had gotten on a different flight, or had leapt to safety from the plane moments before the crash and simply had not gotten in touch with them yet.

Second, individuals begin to bargain with God, telling God all the wonderful things they will do with their life if God would just miraculously restore their loved one to life. People will even give God advice on how such a miracle could be explained to the public if God for some reason does not want the publicity that is likely to occur after miraculously raising someone from the dead.

Third, survivors may experience a wave of anger, trying to blame anyone and everyone, including God and the deceased, for the death. If you are providing psychological support for an individual during this process, take comfort in the likelihood that you may be blamed for the death, but that it is not really anything personal, and the phase will likely pass, and with it the accusation. The grieving individual may, in fact, be terribly embarrassed about such incidents. It is also common for the bereaved to feel terribly guilty for having become angry with God.

Grieving individuals may benefit from someone just being present to them.
Photographer: Euodia Chua.

Fourth, the survivor experiences some degree of depression as the reality of the death hits home. The person begins to think about the range of things that are going to change in life, and the magnitude of the impact, and therefore the sorrow at the personal loss grows.

Another common stage of this process is guilt, as the survivor blames him/herself for the death of the loved one. During this process, the person often reviews every possible thing that could have been done differently in the several days/weeks/months preceding the death to change the outcome, or at least to have made the death more comfortable for the loved one to experience. People often struggle to remember every conversation that took place with the loved one leading up to the death, and think about how things could have been done or said differently.

The final stage of grieving is the development of hope, as the survivor begins to build their new normal life without the physical presence of the deceased loved one. This is the point at which people talk about "moving on," but I think the conceptualization of moving on is unprofitable. It may be more useful to think of grieving as adjusting to the new reality.

Many people have read Kubler-Ross's theory and developed a very simplistic understanding of it. They often think of this as a lock-step progression, with each survivor predictably moving through each stage in the order described previously until the survivor magically emerges from the other side, all better. I may certainly be wrong, but I do not think that Kubler-Ross intended for her work to be understood in this way. Rather, she was trying to explain a general flow of coping procedures that survivors use to deal with the death of a loved one. The fact is, as in so many other things I have discussed earlier in this book, that there are wide individual differences. Not everyone will experience every stage. Not everyone will progress through the stages in order, and, indeed, very few may actually follow this specific flow of stages of grief. People may bounce back and forth from one stage to another as they attempt to resolve their grief. This process can easily take a year or more, despite what mainstream culture in the United States might prefer.

The grieving process may sometimes involve a death, but not the death of a human. Many people's lives may be rocked by the death of a beloved pet. People who have not had a personal or family pet may have difficulty understanding someone actually grieving over a pet. Some individuals may be closer to a pet than to any family member or human friend.

CASE EXAMPLE

One very unusual disaster involved a tremendous explosion of a military resource in the middle of a residential neighborhood, literally in people's yards. Military units had been ordered into the area in the aftermath of the explosion, and the military asked the Red Cross to serve the needs of the local residents.

Many of the military units on patrol were openly bored. They had difficulty understanding what their role was supposed to be. The explosion had clearly been an accident, not a terrorist attack, but the military leadership felt there needed to be a visible military presence because the military had been responsible for the accident.

A psychologist working with the Red Cross was going from door to door meeting with families to offer psychological support. Most residents were functioning well. They had some grief because two military personnel had died in service to their country, but no one they knew had died or even been injured. The violence of the explosion had been traumatic, but people were generally coping well. One family, however, was struggling. Their two young daughters were experiencing significant grief because when the explosion occurred, the family dog had burst out of the house and had not been seen again.

After spending some time supporting the family, the psychologist approached the sergeant leading one of the military units in the area. He told the sergeant that there were two young girls who were struggling because their dog had fled. The sergeant and the soldiers standing around visibly drew themselves up and almost stood at attention. The sergeant asked for a description of the animal, and turned to his men and told them they had a mission. There was a dramatic change in the attitude of the soldiers. News of the search spread through the military units assigned to the response, and they fanned out through the area, searching. Within 2 days the dog was found, and returned to the two excited little girls by a large group of nearly equally excited soldiers, many of whom shed a few tears at the joy of the little girls.

To help individuals work through their grief, offer them an accepting and understanding presence. Try not to judge the reaction of the survivor or to rush them through the process. Be supportive as you listen to the stories of the deceased loved one, often repeated many times. Avoid the common tendency to discourage the person grieving from expressing their emotions. Crying and even weeping may be a useful means of working through grief, and trying to hold all the emotions inside is likely to cause further stress for the individual. This is particularly true for children.

Grief Without Death

Grieving may also occur where no death is involved. The loss of significant possessions may lead to a grieving process. The kind of lost objects that may trigger grieving can sometimes be quite surprising.

The loss of a significant object may be extremely important to a child. Significant objects may have little meaning to adult caretakers in the child's life. It may be a toy, a doll, or a stuffed animal which represents stability to the child. The child may experience the loss of such a significant object as devastating. In the discussion of traumatic events in Chapter 4, I pointed out that if someone experienced an event as overwhelming or traumatic, then for that person the event *was* traumatic, regardless of whether anyone else understood that or not. That is true for children as well. I have often heard parents tell a child who is in the throes of grief over the loss of a significant object, "We'll get you another one. They have others at the local toy store." That response seems logical from an adult point of view. The child, however, may hear that response the same way a bereaved parent feels when someone says, "Well, at least you're young enough to have another one." Sometimes these attempts result in even greater distress in the child, who realizes in the parent's comment that the parent does not understand the child's sense of loss. A better strategy is to comfort the child, to reassure them that things will get better and that the parent will help them through it. A little later, when the child has calmed, the parent's previous strategy may be comforting, asking whether the child would like to pick out another toy. But realize that such a toy will not really be a replacement for what was lost. Adults have significant objects as well, but we generally understand the objects of other adults, and the grieving that their loss may trigger.

The loss of romantic relationships or friendships, the loss of significant opportunities or jobs may also trigger a grieving response. Others may not understand, but that lack of understanding by others does not reduce the grief the individual feels.

Referrals

So if the grieving process is an ordinary response and can reasonably last for a year or more, when might it be best for a CBPFA provider to make a referral for professional support? The suggestions are the same as those noted earlier as general guidelines: It is time to make a referral to a mental health professional when:

1. Unpleasant grief symptoms last more than 4–6 weeks despite good CBPFA support,
2. It becomes difficult for the individual to function effectively on the job, or at home, or at school despite good CBPFA support, or
3. The individual feels concerned about his/her behaviors or emotions, or
4. If you suspect that the individual poses a danger to him/herself or to others, or
5. If you feel that the individual's difficulties are uncomfortably beyond your skill level.

WHEN AND HOW TO REFER

Occasionally over my more than 30 years training doctoral students in clinical psychology, I have encountered a student therapist-in-training who feels that consulting a supervising therapist with a question is a sign of weakness. I shudder at that kind of thinking, and emphatically try to help them learn that getting help in dealing with a difficult circumstance is a sign of strength, not weakness.

When I first came to the University of South Dakota's doctoral Clinical Training Program to interview for a position as an Assistant Professor, I happened to be visiting on a day when there was a client in the program's training clinic who was having a genuine clinical emergency. I was impressed with how comfortably the faculty consulted with each other about how to best handle the situation. The clinical case took priority over classes and my job interview. That impressed me, because that is how I think things should be. I wanted to be a part of that team—a team of highly competent professionals who appreciated the knowledge and skills of their colleagues and were willing to ask their colleagues to look over their shoulders to ensure that only the best care was provided for the individual in need.

Community-Based Psychological First Aid. http://dx.doi.org/10.1016/B978-0-12-804292-2.00011-9

I have been an independently licensed clinical psychologist for more than 30 years. I think I am pretty good at what I do, particularly in disaster situations. But when I run into difficult situations, I still seek consultation with one of my colleagues, or at times with one of my doctoral students, to ensure that I handle that situation in the best way possible. Seeking advice or making a referral is not a sign of weakness, but a sign of personal strength, commitment to excellence, and specifically a dedication to provide the best service possible to those whom we are trying to support.

CBPFA is a powerful tool for providing psychological support. It is not, however, the right tool for every situation. Some people who experience overwhelming events need something more than basic psychological support; they need the assistance of a mental health professional. Sometimes other professionals, such as a medical professional, or a spiritual leader may be a good first step beyond CBPFA. Note, however, that not all spiritual leaders have the training to effectively deal with such referrals, so be certain to check with a spiritual leader before making such a referral.

So when is it best to make a referral to a professional? You may remember the points from Chapter 4 about when it may be best for a professional to be involved:

1. When unpleasant symptoms last more than 4–6 weeks, despite good CBPFA
2. If it becomes difficult for the person whom you are supporting to function effectively on the job, or at home, or at school, despite good CBPFA
3. If an individual feels concerned about his/her behaviors or emotions.
4. If you suspect that a person might pose a danger to him/herself or to others (Note that if the danger seems imminent, it is important to call a law-enforcement official.)
5. If you feel that a client's difficulties are uncomfortably beyond your skill level

Who Would You Go To for Help?

It is most common for individual counties in the United States to have a contract with a community mental health center (CMHC) to provide care for residents of the county. This care is almost always provided with fees based on a sliding scale, that is, the cost of the service is reduced as needed to what the individual can reasonably pay. There are also private and faith-based mental health programs in most areas of the United States. There may also be training clinics at many universities, where graduate students provide therapy under the supervision of licensed mental health professionals, often at little or no cost.

In addition to these traditional mental health resources, primary-care health providers have often been trained to manage mental health crises, and spiritual leaders may also have the necessary training to handle a professional-level crisis intervention.

If the person needing a referral is a child in school, it may also be profitable to involve the school counselor in the situation. Note, however, that although most states require that school counselors be licensed mental health professionals, there are some states in which a school counselor may be someone with no more than a few undergraduate courses in children's mental health. In these cases, however, the counselor is still likely to have the training to get additional assistance for a child in need.

Alarm Bells—When to Worry

Suicide and Self-Harm

If a person threatens to harm her/himself or commit suicide, a referral to a professional truly ***needs*** to be made. A number of studies have recently been published describing suicide as a leading cause of death in the United States, especially among adolescents, young adults (18–24), and among the elderly. This is a problem on a very large scale. It is important that providers of psychological support understand the gravity of such situations and know how to most effectively respond.

There are many myths about suicide, and some of those will be addressed in the current section. One of the most common myths is that people who talk about committing suicide do not do it, so you do not really need to worry if someone threatens suicide. The fact is that about 80% of people who attempt suicide have told someone that they intend to do so, so that myth is patently false. People who talk about suicide often *do* attempt suicide.

Another common response when someone talks about harming him/herself is that the person is just seeking attention. Although it may be true that the individual is seeking attention, it is also true that many people attempt suicide in the process of trying to get someone to help them, and that many of these people die. If someone is that desperate to get attention, it is important that we respond and provide psychological support.

Some of the common phrases that people use to threaten harm to themselves include, "I just want to end it all" and "I just want to go to sleep and never wake up." These are not phrases to dismiss or try to ignore. They are, rather, signs of a desperate need to find comfort in their distress.

It is important to recognize, however, that while 80% of people who attempt suicide have told someone, that also means that 20% of these people *do not* tell anyone. In my PFA workshops, I have often had people approach me at a break after addressing this topic and tell me how grateful they were that I had pointed this out. All of these folks told me that they had experienced the death of a loved one by suicide, and that they had been racking their brains, often for years, trying to figure out why they did not see the suicide coming.

I had a friend years ago who was surrounded by mental health professionals, and was even engaged to one. One day he committed suicide and left behind a diary that revealed that he had a very twisted view of his life, in which he felt that everyone hated him intensely. After his death his friends gathered to discuss his suicide. None of us had any clue about his depression. He portrayed himself as a very happy individual right up until his death. Some people are very effective at hiding their distress. So when someone opens the door to his/her inner life and reveals to you that she/he is considering suicide, it is important that we take advantage of that opportunity and take the steps necessary to maintain the individual's safety. I would have jumped at that chance, but am left with the lingering question of what I could have done that would have made a difference and prevented the suicide of my friend.

Any talk of suicide is something to take seriously. I have fairly often been in groups when someone makes a lighthearted reference to suicide or an indirect comment, such as wanting to go to sleep and never wake up. People often laugh, but I ask the speaker immediately, "Are you thinking about harming yourself or committing suicide?" I want everyone in the group to know that suicide is not something to joke about.

If you think someone might be considering suicide, do not be afraid to ask if that person is thinking about hurting/killing him/herself. I have often heard people say that they do not want to ask about suicide for fear that the question would give the individual the idea of hurting her/himself. A number of years ago, a survey was done of graduating seniors in one state. Almost all of the seniors reported that at some point in the past they had considered suicide. It certainly is not reasonable to assume that these results can be generalized to the entire population, but if nearly all these students had considered suicide before graduating high school, it seems likely that most people in great distress have considered the possibility of suicide. Experts in suicide prevention widely agree that if you think someone may be considering self-harm or suicide, it is always better to ask whether someone is considering suicide, and that there is very little chance that the question could give someone the idea of suicide. The very act of asking someone can help the individual see that someone *does* care, can provide psychological support for the person, and initiate a dialogue that could help to find a more constructive path through the difficult time.

Risky Behaviors

Sometimes individuals who are struggling to cope with overwhelming circumstances engage in risky behavior (ie, actions that pose a significant risk to their lives or the lives of others). The most common of these behaviors is driving at very high rates of speed, often without regard to the consequences for the driver him/herself or anyone else. I recently read an account of a survivor of a vehicle accident that resulted in the deaths of three teenagers. The survivor described an outing that began as a seemingly light-hearted bit of fun by four friends. The driver had been struggling with some life issues, but seemed happy. Once they began to drive, however, he accelerated to extreme speeds on a country road. The survivor recounted that all three of the passengers were screaming for him to stop. But he continued on a bit further before crashing the car, killing himself and two of his three friends.

Was the driver attempting suicide? Perhaps not. When people are overwhelmed by their current situations, sometimes they will engage in risky behaviors. It is generally believed that these individuals are toying with the line between life and death, trying to experience what death might be like, without overtly intending to end their lives. Sometimes, even if inadvertently, the risky behavior results in the death of the person performing the risky behavior, and sometimes results in the deaths of others.

This risky behavior is also seen in some survivors of terrible events; people who have lived through mass casualty incidents or survived a terrible storm or vehicular accident. Such unlikely survival can lead to a phenomenon known as "survivor guilt." I have known survivors of the Nazi concentration camps, soldiers who survived a nearby artillery shell explosion while all the others around were killed, people whose homes were left un-flooded when all their neighbors were under water, and survivors of aviation disasters, all of whom were left questioning, "Why them and not me?" These circumstances sometimes lead to a fascination with the thin line between life and death.

Sometimes risky behaviors endanger not only the individual, but others as well. People may drive at insane speeds on a busy highway or even through a downtown area. Other times these experiences are solitary, such as a man who decided to walk the crown of a very steep barn roof as if on a tightrope. If he had fallen, he probably would have died, but would have been unlikely to harm anyone else.

Whatever the situation, whether only the individual is at risk or others are also endangered, such behavior is a clear indication that the individual would benefit from some professional support. These situations are beyond the need for psychological support that PFA is intended to serve.

Excessive Use of Substances

It is common for people who have experienced an overwhelming event to use alcohol and other drugs to self-medicate and attempt through substances to regulate their traumatic stress. While some might take the position that getting intoxicated is a reasonable response to such extraordinary experiences, it is not very constructive. The use of substances does not solve any problems and often creates more. This is particularly true when individuals drive under the influence or go to work under the influence. I often ask my classes to raise their hands if they have had a friend or family member killed by a drunk driver. Inevitably, nearly every hand in the class is raised. When someone makes excessive use of substances, it is time to consider a referral to a mental health professional.

Threaten Harm to Others

If an individual threatens to harm someone, it is important to take that threat seriously. In the aftermath of a traumatic event, it is very common to see an increase in family violence, including child and spouse abuse. If one considers that both an increase in anger and difficulty in thinking clearly and solving problems are common characteristics of traumatic stress, this increase should not be terribly surprising.

It is important not to dismiss threats a person makes toward you. I have often heard people say that they know the individual threatening them would never hurt them. That is a dangerous assumption. People who are experiencing traumatic stress reactions can do things they might never do in other circumstances. If someone threatens you, take steps to protect yourself, and make a referral for the person making the threat. If the person seems to constitute an immediate threat, it may be best to advise law enforcement of your concerns for the sake of the individual. In most communities law enforcement will do their best to keep the individual safe, while also protecting the public.

Loss of Control

Sometimes people undergoing extreme stress may have difficulty explaining their extreme feelings. One way that this overwhelming sense may be expressed is saying that he or she is losing control. Certainly some people in common conversation may say something similar, simply indicating that it has been a very difficult day. But if someone says this to you, I encourage you to follow up on that comment, just to determine how serious the individual is, and whether she/he might benefit from CBPFA or a referral to a professional.

Many years ago I was working in my office during lunch hour. There was no one else around. An extremely large (not fat, just enormous) man appeared at my open door and asked if he could talk with me. I invited him in and he sat down, and calmly said, "I feel like I'm about to lose control and start killing everyone around me." In any circumstance I would find such a statement quite concerning. What added to my reaction to his statement was that I realized that *I* was the only one around him. As I worked with him I learned that he had very detailed plans and had assembled the tools to kill many people, beginning that afternoon. I did get him additional help, and I will describe that process in a case example in this chapter to illustrate the steps I recommend in getting someone additional help that may be needed.

Withdrawal From Others

If someone begins to withdraw from other people, and that is a change from usual behavior, it may be an indication that the person needs professional assistance. Withdrawal is one of the better predictors of long-term difficulties in resolving traumatic stress. If your efforts to support the person are not effective, PFA may not be the right approach. A professional may be needed to help the individual work through the traumatic stress reaction.

Person is Not in Touch with Reality

If someone is experiencing psychosis, CBPFA is not all the support the person needs. It is important to get a professional involved. You do not need to make psychological diagnoses. In fact, diagnoses are not a part of CBPFA. CBPFA is intended to treat ordinary responses to extraordinary experiences. But if someone does not seem to be in touch with reality, if they have trouble understanding what is going on around them, or if they see or hear things that others do not perceive, it is time to make a referral to a mental health professional.

Any Significant Change in Behaviors

People do not tend to change very much over a short period of time. People's personality traits tend to be very consistent. Theory and research seem to support that personality can change very gradually over a period of many months, but not over the short term, except when an individual has experienced a traumatic event. If you notice that someone you know has started to act very differently, it may be profitable to approach that person and talk with them to see if they have experienced a traumatic event and whether they could use psychological support from you or a mental health professional.

If You Experience Traumatic Stress Symptoms

If a CBPFA provider becomes overwhelmed while providing psychological support, it is an indication that it is time to make a referral to a mental health professional. It is common to experience some stress when supporting others, but if the stress becomes too great, a professional is likely to be more capable of providing the level of psychological support the individual needs.

Basic Principle of Referral

In providing CBPFA, the basic principle for referrals is, "When in doubt, get help from someone else." CBPFA is not intended to deal with every situation. Do not hesitate to get additional help for someone you are supporting.

How to Get Help

There is no one correct way to make a referral, but I recommend several steps.

1. Let the person know that you feel it is necessary to get some additional help. Some fellow mental health professionals suggest not telling someone that you are making a referral. I refer to this as "stealth psychology." I have been a mental health professional for more than 30 years, and I have never had clients become upset when I have told them that I feel that someone

else could do a better job of providing them the support they need. Acting without involving the person whom you are supporting can be perceived as a violation of trust. This is a particular problem if the person whom you are supporting is a family member or friend.

2. Let them know that you care about them. It is useful to make it clear that the reason you want to get someone else involved is that you care about the individual whom you are supporting.

3. Explain the reason for getting help. I think it is profitable to explain to the person why you feel that someone else could provide better support for the individual.

4. Let them know you are still there for them. Try to make it clear that you are not making a referral simply to get rid of them.

5. Give them choices for getting help. If someone is an imminent danger to him/herself or others, this option should be skipped. But when possible, making some of the decisions about how to proceed can help someone regain a sense of control. Some of the choices might include to what professional or agency to make the referral. If you know the local resources, you can offer the individual the choice of which option he/she would prefer. Another option that I try to give is whether the individual wants to go alone or to have me go with them to make the introductions. Another option I try to provide if there is no imminent danger is whether they would like to proceed immediately, or in a little while.

6. Let the person know you are not leaving them. This point is similar to point 4, but it bears repeating. Probably the greatest danger in making a referral is that the individual may feel that you are abandoning them. If you can do so without compromising your own self-care, make it clear that you will continue to be available to them to talk.

7. Let them know you will stay as long as they need you (as long as you are practicing good self-care). This is really an extension of points 4 and 6. The point is that you will continue to be available to provide support in the future. But again, you need to offer this only if it does not risk your own self-care.

8. Let them know you have a relationship now. This may not always be true, and do not say it if you do not feel that it is true. But If you have provided PFA, have listened to their story, and have developed a bond, let them know that you feel that sense of connection with them. It is important that you be genuine in your communication. Do not make this point if you do not feel it is true.

It may help to offer to go with someone you believe would benefit from support by a mental health professional. Photographer: Euodia Chua.

9. Offer to go with them. Having someone else accompany them can give them the courage to reach out and ask for help. Just having someone be present to them in that difficult moment can make a difference.

10. Offer to speak for them if they want. People often tell me that this idea seems strange to them. The importance of it may be clear if you think back on traumatic experiences that may have occurred in your past. For myself, I think of the death of an elder parent. Although I felt fairly comfortable with the death in my mind, I was surprised that when I first told someone about the death, I was suddenly overwhelmed with emotion. Putting things into words can commonly bring on an enormous surge of emotions, and knowing that someone will actually make the initial introduction can reduce the threat of going to a clinic or professional.

CASE EXAMPLE

In the case of the man who came to my office, I told him that I was very impressed that he had used his last ounce of self-control to reach out for help. But as much as I wished I could manage his needs on my own, that I felt that he needed more care than I could provide. I told him that the only way that we could be sure that he and his loved ones were safe was to have him stay for a few days in an inpatient hospital setting.

I further told him that I was required by law in our location to call law enforcement officers to take him there and made sure he understood that he was not being arrested, that they would just make sure he was safe. I told him that when he was finished at the hospital, I would be happy to meet with him and continue our talks, that I appreciated the trust he had placed in me by coming to me for help, and that I was not trying to get rid of him, but wanted to make sure he received the proper care. I was able to offer him a choice of two hospitals. The officers who responded told me they could only transport him to the hospit   that he did not choose. I told the officers that they could tell him themselves if they thought that was important. The two officers looked into the room and saw his size for the first time, then turned back to me and assured me they would transport him to the hospital he had chosen. Because of the situation, I was not able to go with him or speak for him, except to introduce him to the law enforcement officers who would transport him. Despite the very real and imminent danger, the situation worked out very well.

CASE EXAMPLE

A young lady had been walking across campus when she saw a friend sitting by herself under a tree. She stopped to talk to her and saw that her friend seemed very distressed. As they talked, she became more concerned and asked if her friend was considering hurting herself. Her friend shared that she *was* considering suicide and had planned to die that afternoon. The young lady told her friend that she needed help "right now," helped her friend to her feet, and walked across campus to the student psychological services clinic, arm in arm. She then told the director why she had come and introduced her friend to the clinic director. She had acted without any training, just doing what she thought she needed to do, and had done things perfectly right. The clinic director took the woman into a therapy room and determined that the young lady's friend was, indeed, imminently suicidal and had a detailed plan and the means to complete the plan. The director felt certain that the young lady who stopped to talk to her friend had certainly saved her friend's life. The director asked the suicidal woman how long it had been since her friend had stopped to talk to her, and the woman said that it had been about 15 min. The young lady took 15 min out of her day and saved her friend's life.

In Summary

When in doubt… GET HELP! Bring a professional into the picture and ensure that the person whom you are supporting, friend, family, or neighbor, gets the psychological care that they need. PFA is not always adequate to meet people's needs. Sometimes a different set of skills is needed. With a caring and supportive approach, you can facilitate connecting the person in need with the care he/she needs. Through an effective referral, you may genuinely save a life.

TRY THIS

Try to remember whether you have ever considered suicide. What things lead up to that? How did that situation resolve? Were there people you can identify who made a difference in helping you work through that difficult time? How did they do that?

12

PRIVACY AND ETHICAL CONSIDERATIONS

In order for CBPFA to be effective, the people we are supporting must trust both the CBPFA process and the people providing CBPFA. This means that CBPFA is not simply about knowledge and techniques. It is also about keeping faith with those whom you support. This chapter addresses some of these issues and strategies.

Human Value

It is important to value each person as a human being. It would be difficult to find a human being who likes everyone she/he meets. Most people have learned some degree of prejudice against people on the basis of differences in ethnicity, race, country of origin, sexual orientation, religion, or even community. To the extent possible, it is profitable to learn to look beyond the differences between yourself and others, and focus instead on the characteristics we share with others. It is useful to consider our shared humanity.

Carl Rogers, the same theorist who described the essential elements of active listening, wrote extensively about the importance of valuing each person simply for her/his humanity—a concept he called "unconditional positive regard." Rogers maintained that having genuine respect for those whom we serve is absolutely critical to gaining their trust.

When I was an undergraduate student, I worked my way through school, but was only permitted by the university to work in the summers. One of the jobs I held was as the driver of an ice cream truck. I was given an assigned territory where I could sell

Community-Based Psychological First Aid. http://dx.doi.org/10.1016/B978-0-12-804292-2.00012-0

ice cream. Almost the entire area was in the inner city, and the driver on that route had been robbed six times the previous summer. The residents of the area were almost all African-American. On my first day when I finished selling to a group in a housing project, a student I knew from the university approached me. I asked him what he was doing there and he said he lived in the housing project. He told me that if I were smart I would quit the ice-cream job right then. He said there were serious racial issues brewing in the neighborhood, and added that a "white boy" being in the neighborhood every day would not be well-tolerated by the residents. I told him that this was my job for the summer and I planned to keep it. He offered to give me some guidelines for surviving the summer.

His first point was that if I was at all prejudiced against Black or African-American people that I should leave immediately and never come back. He told me that people can sense another person's prejudice either consciously or unconsciously and that they would not only reject my products, but might attempt to harm me. I thanked him for sharing his thoughts with me and told him I thought I would continue. I acknowledged that I probably had some prejudices and stereotypes, but that at my core I respected people of all colors, as my parents had taught me from early childhood.

Later that summer, my route had become the most profitable in the city. A leader of a local street gang tried to take over my route, threatening me with a gun on the street along my route. To my surprise, the crowd around the truck, which the gang member clearly expected to support him, turned on him and drove him away, telling him that I was *their* white boy and *their* ice-cream man. I took their protective attitude toward me, my financial success that summer, and the fact that I was never robbed as a sign that I had effectively communicated my unconditional positive regard to my customers.

The point is that I was not some magical person who had grown up without developing any prejudices or stereotypes. But I did believe that those prejudices were wrong and worked to be respectful to each person I encountered. You can do the same, regardless of your background, and to the extent that you succeed, you will be able to more effectively support a wider range of people.

The first fundamental principle of the Red Cross/Red Crescent Movement is "Humanity." The Red Cross considers basic respect as a human being as one of the fundamental human rights. No human being is more important than another. All are to be treated equally and with respect.

Respecting someone, however, does not mean that you cannot assess the qualities and character of those whom you serve. It is important to ensure your own safety, and to consider whether someone is trying to manipulate you. I may find that I do not like or do not trust a client. But I can still respect that client, and deliver effective psychological support.

Self-Control

Another human value that may be useful to communicate is that each person, at least to some extent, has responsibility for their own dignity, self-respect, and psychological state. There is no question that people and things in the environment can have tremendous impact on one's dignity, self-respect, and psychological state. But, for the most part, those situations are controlling only to the extent that we each allow them to affect us. There are many, many stories of individuals, across the full range of development and age, who have been exposed to overwhelming traumatic events or oppression, and who have maintained a positive outlook, or who were faced with repeated overwhelming demeaning treatment, and who retained an unquestionable dignity and impressive self-respect.

I am reminded of a Lakota friend who was trying to explain to me that "disaster" was not a concept in his culture. He told me, "We see each day as a gift from God. Some gifts are just harder to receive than others." That perspective makes it easier to get through the bad days. Similarly, I spoke with an Islamic woman in the Maldives, who lived on an island completely swept underwater by the December 26, 2004 Indian Ocean tsunami. Her attitude was very positive, although she had lost all her physical possessions in the tsunami. She told me that each day was a gift from Allah, and that for thousands of years her people had made a living from the ocean. She said that the ocean was still there and her people were still there, and that life would go on. The attitude of the entire island was similar. As a result, their community was not depressed, despite having lost literally everything except each other and the ocean surrounding them.

The point is that individuals have some control over whether they become a victim or a survivor, and that is largely a matter of choice. This point is not intended to deny that some stressors can be so overwhelming that traumatic stress results, regardless of how positive one's attitude may be. But as the person recovers it is important for them to realize that they have some degree of control in their recovery, regardless of external forces exerting influence on them.

CASE EXAMPLE

Early in my career, I worked in an addictions treatment center. One young man that I worked with was struggling with the work necessary to recover from his addiction. After a particularly difficult day, the young man shouted, "Well it's not *my* fault I'm an addict!" I calmly handed him a pad of paper and a pen, and told him, "All right, then. You write down the names and addresses of all the people who *are* responsible for your behavior. When you are done, you can leave. Then I will contact them and have them come into treatment. We will send you a letter when you are cured. He looked at me in silence for a long time, then quietly said. "Okay. Let's get down to work."

The principle of self-control also means that the provider is not responsible for the recovery of the person being supported. We support them in their recovery, but they are the ones who recover. Conversely, self-control also means that we are not responsible if a person gets worse. It is up to the providers to be prepared and to do their best. It is up to the person being served by the provider to do the work of recovery.

Ethics

Ethics build on the concept of human value. They are guidelines for protecting those whom we serve as well as ourselves, from harm, either intentional or unintentional.

Privacy

Experience with psychological support programs indicates that maintaining privacy with regard to the discussions that take place is extremely important. It is important that the content of discussions is held private between the people who are directly involved in the discussion. Providers of CBPFA assure those whom they support that their conversations will be kept private. And then they do keep them private.

TRY THIS

Try to remember a time when a friend or a family member revealed to someone a secret you had asked them to keep. How did you feel about that? How did you feel about the person who betrayed your trust? If you have never had that experience, congratulations! Try thinking about a time when you had made an agreement or contract with someone, and that person later broke that agreement or contract. What were your feelings? How long did it take for you to be comfortable interacting with that person afterwards?

Not Taking Advantage

Because of human value, our respect for those whom we serve in CBPFA prevents us from using our relationships to take advantage of those whom we serve. This means that we need to be extremely careful not to exploit those whom we serve, either economically or personally.

> ### CASE EXAMPLE
>
> While working on one disaster I was asked to assign teams of local psychological support workers to go door-to-door offering psychological support to families. One of the workers asked to be assigned to a particular street, explaining that there was a beautiful woman there he had been trying to meet. Another worker asked to be assigned to another specific street, saying that the owner of a local car dealership lived there and the volunteer needed a new car. He was hoping he could get a good deal if he helped the dealer's family. After a short discussion about ethics, both workers were assigned on the opposite side of the city from where they had requested to be.

Sexual Relations

Not taking advantage also means that providers of CBPFA do not take sexual advantage of those whom they serve. That is a fairly easy and straightforward rule for therapists and their clients, and there are restrictions on doing therapy with people with whom the therapist has close personal relationships. But since we are not talking about therapy here, and the whole concept of CBPFA is to provide psychological support to family, friends, neighbors, and colleagues, the issue of sex between providers and clients in CBPFA is not as simple as in therapy. In CBPFA, spouses provide support for one another; lovers care for one another, etc.

The ethical issue that needs to be focused on is not to take advantage of those whom you serve. So one way of thinking about this is that if you did not have a sexual relationship with the person you are serving before you began providing psychological support, it is not ethical to begin such a relationship after you start providing PFA to the person. Even that statement may not hold up to scrutiny, since two people may find that having a caring and supportive relationship will later blossom into a romantic one.

The first principal of psychological support is, "Do no harm." Extensive research on these types of situations has helped make it clear that many times people who choose to have sex with their providers feel at the moment that they are having sex that they are making their own choice to do so. With the passage of time, however, these same people often begin to feel that they have been taken advantage of by the provider they trusted. So even if you care about someone you are serving and they want to have sex with you, if you did not have a sexual relationship with that person before you began providing them with PFA, resist the temptation. A sexual relationship begun under these circumstances is likely to cause difficulty in the relationship later on, and it may disrespect the person's human value. Again, however, that topic may be revisited if months later a long-term romantic relationship has developed.

13

TAKING CARE OF YOURSELF WHILE YOU SUPPORT OTHERS

Following the crash of Flight 232 in 1989, as I have described earlier, one of the national figures responding to that event considered our students total professionals because they knew when to take breaks and refused assignments if they felt the assignment would exceed their ability to cope with the situation. He said that self-care was the most important skill of a professional—if you do not take care of yourself, you cannot take care of anyone else.

I have often been in a leadership role in disaster-relief operations, and many people have commented over the years that they are amazed that I walk away comfortably at the end of my shift and turn my role in the operation over to my colleague designated for that role. I do that so that I can come back the next morning and be effective in leading the operation again. I take breaks periodically, and I eat healthy meals at regular times. These are the same principles that I teach my doctoral students.

Types of Stress

It is important to remember that there are two different kinds of stress that may adversely affect you as you strive to provide psychological support. One is cumulative stress. This stress results from many different stressors. Individually, none of these stressors may be overwhelming. But stress is additive. If you continue to experience stressors, even small ones, without resolving that stress, the stress adds up and can eventually become overwhelming.

Community-Based Psychological First Aid. http://dx.doi.org/10.1016/B978-0-12-804292-2.00013-2

I referred earlier to the proverb about the straw that broke the camel's back. One straw more than the limit the camel can manage is one straw too many. Similarly, if you have experienced all the stress with which you can possibly cope, a single small additional stressor can exceed your coping resources and lead to stress reactions or even psychopathology. We may think that we are not at risk of being overwhelmed by stress because no major stressors have occurred in our lives. But many little stressors can add up and become an overwhelming burden. It is important to be aware of this cumulative stress when we are practicing good self-care.

The other form of stress, traumatic stress, was the topic of Chapter 4. You may recall that this is a form of stress that can overwhelm one's coping skills in an instant. A traumatic event can overwhelm anyone, no matter how strong their coping skills. When you have experienced a traumatic event, it is important to be vigilant and both closely monitor your own stress reactions and aggressively practice self-care.

Prevention of and Self-Care for Cumulative Stress

The best way to practice good self-care for cumulative stress is to effectively cope with even minor stressors as they occur in your life. There are many tired jokes by comedians and television sitcoms about marriages failing because of the way one spouse squeezes the toothpaste tube, or because one spouse does not take out the garbage. But it has been striking to me how often cumulative stress has been the major source of difficulty in couples or families having problems in their relationships. It has been very common in my clinical experience for couples and families to come for therapy complaining about a very minor conflict which they say is threatening their relationship.

CASE EXAMPLE

In one couples therapy case, the wife met with me first in therapy and said they had been married for some time. From her perspective, the relationship had been heavenly until one recent morning when her husband sat down to breakfast, pounded his fist on the table, said he could not take it anymore, and walked out of the house. She had not seen him since then until he came into the waiting room for the couple's therapy session. She said she genuinely had no idea what had caused his outburst and departure. I then interviewed the husband privately before the three of us had a session together. I asked him to explain the problem from his perspective. He began with, "Well nine months ago…".

I knew immediately the kind of story that would unfold. His wife had made a particular dish for breakfast for him one morning shortly after they returned from their honeymoon. He disliked it, but when his wife asked him how it was, "rather than hurt her feelings" he told her it was wonderful. Delighted with his reaction, the wife had made the same dish every morning for the past 9 months. The husband had never said anything to her because he did not want to offend her! But the stress built up to the point that he separated from his wife, and this minor stressor over time had nearly destroyed their marriage. Some fairly simple work on communication, and learning that dealing with the minor discomfort involved in resolving minor conflicts prevents major cumulative stress helped them to begin healing their relationship.

Self-care for providers of PFA is most effective if it focuses on prevention. The day-to-day hassles of life need to be resolved as soon as practically possible. If one deals with the small stressors as they occur, there will be no opportunity for cumulative stress to rear its ugly head. I refer you back to Chapter 8 to examine strategies for coping with stress. I would also suggest that it is very good strategy to make use of the strategies this book endorses—CBPFA. Practice what we preach… This is particularly important when we have allowed the cumulative stress to build in our lives. The greater the accumulation, the more important it is to formally cope with that stress.

Traumatic Stress and Secondary Stress

Secondary stress is a fairly simple idea. It means that helpers can experience a form of traumatic stress as a result of listening to the stories of those whom they are serving. It is essentially a specific form of cumulative stress. When PFA providers support many people, especially those who were directly exposed to a traumatic event, they hear many different tales of people's suffering and/or stress. Sometimes providing psychological support through active listening can lead to the provider experiencing some of the same symptoms as the people having traumatic stress reactions, those whom the provider is supporting.

This is not a new phenomenon. There are many terms for this, including "vicarious traumatization." Secondary stress is characterized by signs and symptoms similar to those displayed by people who directly experienced the traumatic event. These include: emotional symptoms such as anxiety, anger, and depression; cognitive symptoms such as nightmares, cynicism, difficulty making decisions, and intrusive images often based on the stories heard about the event; physiological problems such as stomach upset or diarrhea, and behavioral symptoms such as having no time or energy for oneself, disconnection from loved ones, and general social withdrawal. There are other characteristics that may not fit easily into a single category, such as failure to practice good self-care.

The risk of secondary stress is increased for workers who have other stressful events taking place in their lives or have a history of traumatic events in their lives—remember that stress is additive. Risk is also increased if providers are relatively inexperienced and if the providers are resistant to receiving psychological support from others.

CASE EXAMPLE

Mass casualty disasters are typically one of the most difficult types of disasters for relief workers. On one mass casualty response, a volunteer from a city in the next state was completing the paperwork of joining the disaster relief operation. We were talking casually as the administrative matters were done. The worker told me that they had volunteered for this relief operation because the stress from their job had been becoming unbearable. I was concerned and explained that mass casualty disasters were very stressful. The worker assured me that the change from the daily stress at their workplace would make it easy to deal with the mass casualty disaster. The worker needed to be admitted to a psychiatric hospital 3 days later, having become overwhelmed with cumulative stress.

The way to prevent secondary stress is to practice good self-care (see Chapter 8), actively seek support from your family and friends, and build good teamwork and collaboration with other CBPFA providers.

Family Stress

It is also important to realize that your secondary stress can affect your family. If you are experiencing significant stress, you are likely to change your way of interacting with your family. Many of the symptoms of secondary stress interfere with good social interaction. It is important, therefore, that you monitor family stress, and work to quickly resolve stress that arises. Beware of cumulative stress in your family. Create in your family a clear understanding that it is okay to talk about stress and tension within the family. That is the easy part. The hard part is actually having comfortable and open discussions when somebody in the family is unhappy, or uncomfortable with what is taking place. It may also be useful to offer to family members to have someone outside the family provide CBPFA if the family would prefer.

Recognizing Long-Term Effects of Traumatic Events

It is important for you to understand that high levels of long-term stress can have significant negative consequences. If cumulative stress builds to high levels for a long period of time, or traumatic stress remains unresolved for long periods, significant stress symptoms may develop.

Most of these long-term symptoms are similar to the symptoms of traumatic stress, but are often more severe. They commonly include sleep disturbances ranging from various forms of insomnia to the opposite end of the spectrum, sleeping too much. There may also be problems with anxiety, anger, and depression. Excessive use of substances such as alcohol or illegal drugs is also common.

But there are also some symptoms that are primarily associated with the long-term effects of stress. Perhaps the most unusual (and most extreme) of these symptoms is anhedonia, a total lack of ability to experience pleasure. There may also be numbing of other emotions—a less extreme but more generalized response than anhedonia. Personality change can also occur, as well as changes in belief systems.

It is also common for individuals with prolonged high levels of stress to experience physical complications, including diffuse physical symptoms such as aches and pains, loss of appetite, and general lack of energy. Such symptoms are the most frequent cause of people seeking help for their prolonged stress. Stress causes strain on various organ systems in the body. Various studies have reported that prolonged stress results in increased rates of infectious diseases, and cardiovascular, neurological, and gastrointestinal problems, cancer, and shorter life expectancy.

When to Seek Professional Support

The "rules of thumb" described in Chapter 4 apply equally to you as to those whom you support. It may be time to seek some professional assistance when:

1. Unpleasant symptoms last more than 4–6 weeks despite good CBPFA support,
2. It becomes difficult for you to function effectively on the job, or at home, or at school despite good CBPFA support, or
3. You feel concerned about your behaviors or emotions, or
4. If you suspect that you may be a danger to yourself or to others.

TRY THIS

It can be a profitable exercise to sit down and think about what signs or symptoms in yourself tell you that you are becoming uncomfortably stressed and need to focus on self-care. For some people, it is becoming more irritable or having trouble sleeping. Others describe specific aches or pains. Some say that becoming less organized is their cue, or watching television or reading without any memory of the content of those activities. Try to make a list of your personal signs that stress is becoming too strong. Then, make a list of your favorite ways of reducing your stress. What activities do you find soothing and renewing? It is good to keep both of these lists in mind. Learn to recognize cumulative stress in its early stages, and make sure to work at your self-care to reduce it.

14

CHILDREN AND TRAUMATIC STRESS

Community-Based Psychological First Aid. http://dx.doi.org/10.1016/B978-0-12-804292-2.00014-4

The discussions of stress and reactions to stress in the book thus far have been focused on adults. But whether you are going to provide PFA to friends and family or to your community, it is likely that some of those whom you support will be children and adolescents. In supporting these younger persons, it is important to understand how their reactions may differ from those we commonly experience in adults. As with adults, children's reactions to traumatic stress are generally grouped into four categories: emotional, physical, behavioral, and cognitive.

Children's Emotional Reactions to Traumatic Stress

As with adults, the primary emotional reaction to traumatic events in children is anxiety. But in children, anxiety often takes the form of a feeling of vulnerability. Children often have a fear that the traumatic event will happen again, and although adults may have similar fears, children feel freer to talk about their fears than most adults. Children's feelings of vulnerability may also become obvious as a fear of being left alone. This is more likely to occur if the family was separated during the event. Adults often feel that the child's fears are exaggerated or "silly," but it is interesting to note that other children will judge the child's fears as reasonable.

This vulnerable feeling is often described as a "loss of a sense of safety" by mental health professionals. After the 1995 bombing of the Murrah Federal Office Building in Oklahoma City, the American Red Cross (together with the American Psychological Association, AT&T, and the Disaster Mental Health Institute) conducted a national telephone hotline for children affected by the bloody scenes broadcast by national networks. Children from 34 states called the "Helping the Children Heal" hotline. Some of the Red Cross volunteer disaster mental health professionals who staffed the hotline were amazed that some of the children who called used similar words, saying, "I just don't feel safe anymore."

Children, like adults, also experience sadness and depression, as well as anger (although the anger is often expressed in more subtle ways than adults) following a traumatic event. Another common emotional response among children is guilt. Although adults may experience survivor guilt, as described in Chapter 11, children often have a sense that the traumatic event was somehow their fault. Children live in a world in which many adults do not believe them. If something is missing, the child is often accused of taking it, and no amount of denial may change that adult accusation. If something is broken, it is often assumed that the child did it. If children say something an adult does not believe, they are often told to stop lying. Children, then, often learn to take responsibility for whatever goes wrong. They tend to trust responsible adults, and although they do not understand it, they often come to believe that bad things that happen really *are* their fault. If it were not their fault, why would the adults whom they love be telling them repeatedly that it *is* their fault? When a traumatic event happens, children and adolescents often fear that somehow this terrible thing was their fault.

CASE EXAMPLE

When I was consulting in Sri Lanka after the 2004 Indian Ocean Tsunami, a young boy approached me and apologized for having caused the tsunami. Although I am not permitted to do direct interventions when I am in another country (because of international guidelines), I felt that I could not let this little boy's statement go unanswered. I thanked him for his apology, told him that I was amazed by his powers, and asked him what other weather he could control. He looked at me curiously and said that he could not control any other kind of weather. I asked him why, then, he thought that he had caused the tsunami. He thought for a moment, and thoughtfully replied, "Maybe I *didn't* cause the tsunami." Imagine carrying the burden of that guilt, of fearing he had caused the deaths of vast numbers of people, and the destruction of every village the boy had probably ever known.

Children's Physical Reactions to Traumatic Stress

Children are far more likely than adults to express their stress reactions in physical symptoms. Like adults, children experience a wide variety of physical symptoms. Compared to adults, however, children tend to complain more of headaches and stomachaches. This may be because children have more difficulty in localizing and describing pain than adults. Children are also more likely to have eating problems, which may actually be an indication of gastrointestinal problems (eg, nausea, intestinal cramps, and diarrhea).

Children's Cognitive Reactions to Traumatic Stress

Children's general cognitive functioning (their thinking ability) may be reduced by traumatic stress reactions, resulting in confusion and even disorientation. This is likely to be a particularly difficult symptom for school-age children. More specifically, they often experience difficulty in concentrating and making good decisions. This may often appear as behavioral problems in the classroom. Children who are having difficulty focusing are more likely to have problems staying on-task and are more likely to misbehave.

Conversely, school may be the place where children function best when having a traumatic stress reaction. For some children the structure and predictability of the school day provide a sense of order, which a child may find comforting. Similarly, the ability to complete classroom or homework assignments may help the child to gain a sense of control in the midst of a chaotic situation.

Children's Behavioral Reactions to Traumatic Stress

Perhaps the most frequently described behavioral reaction to traumatic stress in children is "regressive behavior." This technical term basically means that children may act younger than their chronological age. For example, a 4-year-old may act more like a 3-year-old. It is important to understand that this is often not deliberate misbehavior or acting out. Rather, it is an ordinary reaction to an extraordinary situation. Children who have learned to live without diapers may again need them. Children even to the age of high school students may take on characteristics from much earlier in life, exhibiting insecurity and clinginess.

Bedtime problems are also a frequently cited behavioral reaction in children. This may take the form of difficulty falling asleep at night or awakening during the night and having trouble getting back to sleep, just as happens in adults. But children often also develop significant fear of the dark, and fear that the traumatic event will happen again during the night. This is especially true following traumatic events that actually did occur at night.

Trigger Events

The traumatic stress reactions described previously may not be immediate, and may be delayed by months, as is true in adults. Various smells, sights, and sounds may be the triggers for these traumatic stress reactions. It can be useful to identify these triggers, to help children avoid them. But these triggers often are not obvious. Children's stress reactions may also serve as triggers for renewing the traumatic stress symptoms in adults.

Risk Factors—Individual

There are many characteristics of children's experiences that may make them more vulnerable to traumatic stress reactions. The wide variety of these risk factors accounts for the wide range of individual differences in response to traumatic events.

Coping Resources Unavailable

After a traumatic event, adults are often consumed with work that needs to be done to restore things to their former state. Their energies are focused on their own and/or their families' survival. Because of this, parents and other caretakers (eg, teachers, relatives, babysitters, spiritual leaders) may not be available to children to provide them with support, and just at a time when the children may have their greatest need for support.

Some people are surprised to learn that school can be a significant source of support for children. If school is not in session, whether because of the traumatic event or the season of the year, favorite teachers and friends important to the child are unavailable, making coping more difficult.

Age and Developmental Phase

The age and developmental phase of the child are also important to the vulnerability of the child and are keys in the types of symptoms children may exhibit. Cognitive development is necessary to understand both traumatic events and the consequences of those events. Later in this chapter, I will present further details about developmental phases.

Poor Health

If a child has been in poor health, this increases the chances of having difficulty with a traumatic stress reaction. Whether the child suffers from chronic poor health or has suffered a recent significant illness, the child's defenses are weakened and coping resources may have been significantly reduced due to fighting the illness. In addition, in cases in which the illness is ongoing, treatment and medications for the condition may not be available in the chaos that often follows traumatic events such as major disasters.

Similarly, children with physical difficulties are at increased risk in disasters. Debris scattered about in a disaster may make it harder for children with physical difficulties to move around, and their risk of additional injury in increased compared with an able-bodied child. As with illnesses, there may be additional difficulty in receiving routine treatment after a disaster. Children who have disabilities that make it difficult for them to express themselves are at particular risk. We think this is because it is more difficult for them to discuss and effectively process their experiences after a disaster.

Pre-event Stress

A child who has been having a particularly high amount of stress before a disaster is more likely to have greater levels of stress after a disaster occurs than a child who was not very stressed before the disaster. Remember the earlier discussion of Spielberger's model of individual reactions to stress—when a child is already stressed, the child is more likely to find new events stressful. And stress is additive; the stress resulting from a disaster is just added on to the stress that already existed before the event.

Stressors that increase difficulty for children include recent family stress such as parents getting divorced, a newly blended family, or the birth or adoption of a sibling. Even when these experiences are positive overall, they still require a significant amount of mental energy as the child strives to build an understanding of the new family relationships that result. Mental energy devoted to these pre-existing situations is energy that is not available to cope with the aftermath of a disaster or other traumatic event. Children who have recently started school or are having difficulty in school may have difficulties similar to children experiencing family stressors.

Previous Traumatic Experiences

Having previously experienced traumatic events can sometimes be helpful to a child, and in other situations it can be more stressful. Children who have successfully coped with traumatic events in the past are likely to have more effective strategies for dealing with a new traumatic event, and likely to have more self-confidence in their ability to handle the situation. On the other hand, for children who are still struggling with previous traumatic events, the new traumatic event simply becomes added stress and makes coping all the more difficult.

Coping Skills

The level of a child's coping skills is very important (although remember that traumatic events by definition can overwhelm anyone's coping skills, no matter how strong). But the type of coping that a child prefers can also predict greater difficulties. Some children use structure to help them cope with stress in their lives. That is, children who find comfort in order and predictability in their daily lives are more likely to experience difficulties in coping with the aftermath of a traumatic event.

Expectations of Self and Others

A significant possible source of stress for a child is what the child is *expected* to do in a situation. In mainstream American culture, the oldest child in a family is often expected to take on a more significant role than other children in the family. This is especially true if adults in the family were injured or killed in the event. The older sibling may be asked to take on more responsibility for the care of younger siblings. And this comes at a time when the younger siblings need more attention and care because of their own stress in the situation, and when the older sibling may also be feeling significantly increased stress.

These expectations may be placed on the child directly by adults. I have heard an adult say to a child about 11 years old whose father was injured in an event, "Well, you'll have to be the man of the family now." Think of the pressure such expectations can put on a child! How does an 11-year-old boy know how to be the man of the family, particularly in the chaotic situation that can follow a traumatic event? Other times children may place these expectations on themselves, forcing themselves to take on more and more responsibility because they feel that is the right thing to do. Although this may seem noble, it may also put the child at greater risk of having a traumatic stress reaction.

Children also have expectations of their parents and other caretakers. Children tend to monitor their parents' behavior fairly closely after traumatic events. They can often tell when parents are experiencing high levels of stress or very strong emotions. Children may experience increased stress just by recognizing the traumatic stress reactions of adults around them. Children may interpret a traumatic stress reaction in their caretakers as more significant than it actually is. And at the same time, those adults may be less available to support the child, resulting in an increasing spiral of stress.

Status of Family Members

If family members are missing, injured, or dead as a result of the event, children may have much higher levels of stress. This may be true even if everyone in the family is fine, but the family was not together when the event occurred (eg, children in school, or parents at work), or were separated during an evacuation. The idea of "women and children first" may sound noble, but is likely to result in much higher levels of stress in the children involved than if family units are evacuated together.

Ethnic, Religious, and Cultural Factors

Children who are not comfortable communicating in the dominant local language are likely to experience greater stress following a traumatic event. Difficulty in understanding instructions, in communicating one's concerns, or in asking questions makes situations more difficult. I have found in my travels that even if I can successfully ask a question in the local language, I often cannot understand the response.

If a family's language is different from the local language, children in the family are the most likely among the family members to speak the local language. Many times a child becomes the interpreter for the family following a traumatic event. This often results in the child translating the parents' descriptions of the family's losses and the parents' concerns to disaster relief agencies. In disaster-relief operations I have often seen the eyes of a child who had been thrust into such an interpreter role grow wider with fear as the child translated, and heard from the parents' perspective how much trouble the family was in as a result of the traumatic event.

Similarly, children who have recently immigrated or even simply moved to a new neighborhood are likely to be at greater risk for traumatic stress reactions. It takes time to build a social support network in a new neighborhood, especially if the new location is dramatically different culturally from their former residence. In addition, the child needs to develop a new cognitive framework for understanding the new home—a sort of cognitive map of areas to play, where it is safe to go, where friends are located, etc. Even the land, trees, animals, and even vehicles on the street may look different from where the child previously lived. This cognitive process of coming to understand a new home takes a large amount of mental energy, and that makes less energy available for coping with the traumatic event.

Child's Perception and Interpretation of the Event

Earlier in the chapter, I described how children can sometimes feel that they caused a traumatic event, usually by a "bad" thought or behavior. This can place a great burden on a child and dramatically increase the stress of the situation. Therefore, when providing psychological support for a child it is important to ask the child to describe their thoughts about the event. Unfortunately, children who believe they are responsible for an event often carry that burden as a shameful secret. They may be hesitant to reveal it to you because they feel ashamed of what they feel they have done. But if you create a safe environment and invite the child to talk about the event, the child may take the opportunity to unburden him/herself of secret feelings of responsibility.

Risk Factors—Event

Just as characteristics of individuals can affect how stressful an event may be for a child, characteristics of events also make the events more or less stressful. Understanding these factors may help you to know which events may be more troublesome for a child. The event characteristics that may be significant for a child are much the same as for adults. I will try not to repeat the discussion of event characteristics in Chapter 5, but address more how these characteristics may have particular impact on children.

Sudden and/or Prolonged Disasters

Disasters that occur suddenly with little advance warning are more difficult for children, as is true for adults. But having advance warning, such as in a hurricane or slow-rising flood may also be very stressful. Children *can* prepare for an event, but it is not safe to assume that a child *has* prepared for an event just because there has been advance warning. In fact, sometimes the frantic preparation of adults may be very unsettling for a child, and make it harder for the child to prepare for the event. The abrupt changes that a child may experience after a traumatic event make the situation more difficult, changes such as differences in the appearance of a neighborhood due to storm damage, flood waters being where the child thinks of the land being dry, or suddenly living in a shelter without privacy and without many of the personal things the child is used to and in which the child takes comfort.

Natural/Technological Events

As discussed in Chapter 5, adults generally find technological disasters more stressful than natural disasters. For younger children, however, natural disasters are likely to be more stressful. Children have developed some concepts about how the world works. The earth is solid. Water flows in the river. Storms can be scary, but usually do not hurt us. My house is solid and strong and safe. Natural disasters often violate those concepts of the world. Earthquakes turn the land we walk on into a scary moving surface.

(Having experience a moderate earthquake recently, I can relate to that!) Floods cause waters to sweep through residential areas. Storms can destroy entire neighborhoods. Houses can be ripped apart in an instant by a tornado or hurricane. Natural disasters often have more visual impact than technological disasters. A certain level of cognitive development is required to understand something such as the air being poisonous because of a chemical leak, or to understand the horror of a plane crash.

As adolescents develop more cognitive sophistication they are also more likely to respond to disasters like adults, seeing technological disasters as more stressful than natural disasters.

Continuing Threat

Children often find events more threatening when the danger persists or occurs repeatedly. After Hurricane Andrew in Florida in 1992 the weather returned to a more typical pattern, with thunderstorms occurring almost every afternoon. Many of the children who resided in the devastated area south of Miami had huddled in their homes through the night as the winds of the hurricane destroyed their homes and vast areas around their homes. The daily thunderstorms that followed the hurricane were often accompanied by children screaming with fear that the hurricane had come back again. It does not help that we give hurricanes names, which leads some children to think of them as evil beings out to get them.

Earthquake aftershocks may be particularly terrifying for children. In Gujarat, India following the catastrophic 2001 earthquake, aftershocks continued for many months, frightening children and adults alike. In one sad incident, the impact of those fears was dramatically demonstrated. One morning during a school day a very heavy truck traveled through one of the affected villages. The truck rumbled, and its passing weight caused the school building to tremble. Children feared that the earthquake was happening again and panicked. A dozen children died in the stampede that followed.

Time of Onset

It is quite common for children to fear the dark. Like adults, children often find events that occur at night much more threatening.

Personal Losses

Death or injury of, or even separation from family members during an event greatly increases the stressfulness of an event. Damage to a child's home is often much more stressful than might seem reasonable to an adult. But it is the damage to the child's concept of the world that causes the major stress. Homes are supposed to be safe and strong. When the home is damaged in a disaster the child begins to question his or her other concepts of the world.

Similarly, as described in Chapter 10, the loss of some possession in an event can be very upsetting for a child. Parents often dismiss these reactions as exaggerated or "silly," perhaps assuring the child the parent will get another one for the child. But even though parents may see a child's reaction to the loss of some toy as overblown or ridiculous, other children often see the reaction as totally reasonable. It seems that to children one possession may represent all the things that they have, and the loss of one item means that everything else may be lost just as easily.

Seeing/Hearing/Smelling an Event

The sensory experiences of the scene after a traumatic event can be very powerful for a child. Prolonged exposure to someone injured or killed in the event when a child is trapped in debris, for example, can be extremely difficult for a child. Similarly, hearing the cries of children and adults injured in the event or merely frightened can be very difficult. But the sounds and sights of the event itself can be very difficult, and create lasting traumatic memories. Children may be especially moved by the sight of an injured child. In the bombing of the Murrah Federal Building in Oklahoma City in 1995, live television coverage showed recovery workers bring out the bloodied bodies of dead children and horribly injured children from the rubble. The volume of parents calling Red Cross chapters across the nation to ask for help in assisting their children in coping with these images led to the "Helping the Children Heal" telephone hotline discussed earlier in this chapter.

The Importance of Individual Differences

As with adults, it is important to remember that there is a tremendous variety of individual differences in children's reactions to traumatic events. I have tried to describe some of the more significant individual and event variables that influence these individual reactions. It is important to realize that it is perfectly normal for two children to have very different reactions to the same event, or for an individual child to react very differently to two events that seem very similar. It is also important to remember that reactions to traumatic events may be significantly delayed after the event, sometimes beginning months after the event.

Challenges in Working with Children

Even very caring and supportive parents may not be aware of their child's difficulties in coping with a traumatic event. Parents may feel overwhelmed by their own process of coping with the event. Sometimes parents simply deny to themselves that their child is struggling with the event, perhaps because the parents do not have the psychological resources left to cope with their child's difficulty. It is also true that a child's reactions are often not what parents expect them to be.

CASE EXAMPLE

One parent told me that her 8-year-old son had fallen and suffered a severely broken leg, with the jagged edge of the broken bone poking out of his leg. She called an ambulance, and when it arrived her son was screaming intensely. He was inconsolable and even unable to speak. When they arrived at the hospital he began to calm down and the mother told her son that the doctors would ease his pain. Able to speak again, her son explained that he was not crying because of the pain, but because he was terrified of ambulances!

The truly unfortunate result of parents not recognizing their child's psychological struggle with a traumatic event is that the lack of understanding from the parent or other adult in the child's life increases the stress still further, as the child realizes that the adults on whom the child relies for support do not even understand what the child is experiencing.

Differences in Developmental Stages

In this section, I will present a brief description of some of the characteristics of children of particular age groups. Please keep in mind that these are broad descriptions and not intended to represent any individual child's response. Individual children may quite ordinarily function slightly above or below their chronological age, so even if you are interested in just learning about the developmental stage of one child, it may be profitable to learn the characteristics of children younger and older than the specific child in whom you are interested.

Birth–2 Years of Age

Children at this age are likely to have little cognitive understanding of what is taking place in the aftermath of a traumatic event. They can, however, sense differences in the reactions of their primary caretakers, and may react to the stress reactions of adults and siblings in their lives. At this age verbal communication is rather limited. Cognitive images may not be well-developed at this age, but it is generally believed that children at this developmental stage can retain what are probably fairly vague memories of images, sounds, smells, and physical sensations. Generally, stress reactions in this age range are characterized by increased irritability and a desire for more physical contact with caregivers.

Ages 2–6 Years (Preschool)

Preschool children generally lack highly developed verbal and cognitive skills, and are not likely to be able to effectively cope for themselves. They are likely to rely on adults for comfort. They are strongly influenced by the reactions of adults and other family members. Fear of abandonment is commonly a significant reaction, particularly if there has been a death of a family member or a pet. They may be quite clingy. Preschool children will sometimes have enough cognitive development to develop a sense of their own vulnerability. This, in turn, sometimes leads to intense fear. The cognitive development of children in this age range often means that the irreversibility of some losses literally cannot be understood. For example, a parent may patiently explain that a family member has died. The child may sit and listen intently and indicate understanding. But then may ask whether the deceased family member will be home for dinner. This is also a common age for the magical thinking that leads children to think they are responsible for the event.

Toddlers may act out their view of the event repeatedly. Following a flash flood, for example, a toddler may use building blocks to create a "town" and then have a "flood" rush through and destroy the buildings. This is generally seen as an attempt by the child to gain an understanding of what has taken place, and this play may go on for hours.

Regressive behaviors are common in this age group, with some children returning to bedwetting, thumb sucking, and clingy and dependent reactions. It is certainly easier to say than to do, but the best response to such behaviors is patient understanding, and soothing assurances of safety and security. There is generally little need to be concerned about these behaviors unless they last more than 4–6 weeks. If these behaviors last that long, it may be profitable to have the child see a mental health professional who specializes in children, so that the professional can assist the child in working through their reactions.

Ages 6–11 Years (School Age)

The cognitive development in this age range generally enables children to begin to understand the permanence of losses, including death. These children are also better able to understand the issues surrounding a traumatic event. They may be intensely focused on learning details of the event, trying to grasp more thoroughly what has taken place. Such preoccupation may interfere with school performance.

Regressive behavior is common. Children at this age who are coping with a traumatic event are likely to compete for attention both at home and school. They may be irritable and aggressive, even if this is very uncharacteristic of their usual behavior. Nightmares are common. Children may avoid school, often because they are struggling with being able to pay attention in class. Social withdrawal may occur. Children in this age group may be frightened of loud noises, and have very high activity levels. Stress in these children often leads to many physical complaints (eg, headache, stomachache, muscle pain).

Ages 11–18 Years (Pre/Adolescent)

With increasing age in this group, reactions are likely to be more similar to those of adults. Stress reactions can be confusing at this age, because at times a child may have reactions more like an adult, and at other times more like a child. With increasing age, dangerous, risk-taking behavior may be seen. Older children may struggle to understand the relationship between life and death. Sexual promiscuity sometimes accompanies traumatic stress in this age group, even in children for whom such behavior seems unthinkable to parents. Some child specialists believe that in these ages children may begin to understand that life can be fragile and short, leading to a desire to experience everything that life has to offer. On the other hand, children in this age group may withdraw and lose interest in peer activity.

Individual Differences

At the risk of repeating it too often, it is important to recognize that each child is unique and is likely to respond in individual ways, even within the same age group.

Strategies for Supporting Children

It is important to keep in mind that the reactions described previously are ordinary reactions to extraordinary events. If a child's reactions fall within the framework described above, try to help the child understand that these are acceptable and "ordinary" reactions when coping with a difficult time in life. Try to be patient with children's reactions. Some reactions such as irritability, or repeated questions about the event can be frustrating for others.

Sometimes adults tell children that the children's fears are silly or even stupid. This is not likely to help a child, and may drive a wedge between the child and the adult. The child knows that the fears themselves are real, even if they are not realistic, and whether or not the adult understands. An alternate strategy to provide support is for the adult to accept a child's fears within a discussion of what is likely to happen. For example, a child may be afraid that a tornado will come back to attack her/his home again. A good response might be to say, "Well, I certainly understand why you might be afraid that would happen. It *is* possible that another tornado could happen here again, but the one that struck our town is all gone and cannot come back. There is very, very little chance that another tornado will strike here for a very long time." This accepts the child's fear, but also points out why she/he can try to feel less scared.

Sometimes psychological support for children is best provided while playing with them. Photographer: Tyler Bradley.

TRY THIS

If you are a parent or grandparent, try this with your own children. If you do not have children, get permission from the parents of nieces or nephews, or from friends who have children. Try sitting down and talking with children of various ages about how they think storms happen. Where do they come from? What causes them? How do they feel about them? It is often best to have such discussions while playing with them. Alternatively, if your family has experienced a recent disaster or traumatic event, try gently giving them encouragement to talk about the experience and how they think about it.

A child's lack of understanding is the foundation for the greatest fears. Therefore, when supporting children, try to help them understand in a developmentally appropriate way what happened and what is likely to happen in the near future. Help children understand what caused a natural disaster. Provide simple, accurate information. *Listen* to what children say, especially to their questions. They are often telling you what they need to know to feel more comfortable. Answering their questions or gently clarifying their thinking may be a great help to them.

Even by early primary school, children sometimes fear that their traumatic stress reactions are a sign that there is something wrong with them. This is fairly logical, since the children are unlikely to have experienced anything like it before. It may be helpful to share with a child that adults were afraid during the event too, or that adults find it hard to cope with the conditions after the event: "I understand why you want to go back to our house. I'd sure like to go back too. But right now the storm has damaged our house, and we have to fix it before we can go back. That may take a few (days, weeks, months). Until then, what can we do to make staying here in the shelter more fun?" This can help children feel more comfortable with their reaction. But do not share painful details of your or other adults' reactions. I have heard adults talking to very young children and sharing that the adults had been afraid too. So far so good… but then the adults start to talk about their fears in detail, describing their nightmares, or their fears about what could happen next time. Children listening to such adults are liable to wind up more terrified than before the adults tried to help them.

Conversely, children may sense that adults are struggling with the aftermath of a traumatic event. If the adults deny their feelings, children may feel that the event is so terrible that even the adults cannot talk about it.

It is useful to realize that children generally do not recover from traumatic stress reactions until after their parents or caretakers do. Therefore, if you encounter a child having a traumatic stress reaction, think about what the rest of the child's family may need as well. If you are a parent, let this be good motivation to work on your own self-care and recovery. That is likely to also help your child(ren) recover.

Preparation

Having children participate in preparing for disasters can also be comforting to them. For younger children it may be as simple as making sure that flashlights for an emergency kit work, whereas older children may be able to assemble items on a checklist and put them in a storage container. At any age, school children can participate in family disaster drills, learning what to do if the smoke alarm goes off, or if there is an earthquake, for example.

As I described earlier, it is important to help children understand what causes natural disasters, and to understand what things can be controlled, and what things are simply out of human control. This includes an understanding of how preparedness can help respond to a disaster, and in some cases even reduce the impact of the disaster. Such activities can help provide a child with a sense of some control over potential disasters. Remember to make sure that the activities are age-appropriate for the child.

Returning to a "New Normal"

For school-age children, particularly, it may be helpful to organize play sessions with their friends. Disasters often result in families being displaced and schools not operating for a period of time. Helping children reconnect with their friends can sometimes be a significant reassurance for the child that not *everything* has changed. It is also likely to be useful to help your child participate in peer group activities in which they were involved before an event, once those activities begin to happen again.

Gently encourage a child to talk about their experience of the event and its aftermath. It is probably best not to pressure children to talk about the event before they are ready. But you can let them know periodically that, "When you feel like talking about what happened, I'm ready to listen to you." And, of course, then you need to truly be ready to sit down and listen when they are ready to talk.

Some children may talk about their experience in the event over and over. If the child seems to be stuck in this cycle of behavior, it may be helpful to divert the child's attention to other topics. This can be done very gently, and never needs to be done forcefully.

It may be profitable to encourage children to participate in structured, nondemanding activities such as community cleanup activities. In Sri Lanka after the 2004 tsunami, one of the psychosocial support programs hired the surviving local children to clean up some of the extensive litter and debris along the road left by the 90-ft. wave. Younger children were asked to just pick up litter and put it in containers. Older children were given other age-appropriate roles. This was not child labor, but an encouragement for the children to get active and participate in the community's recovery. Children not only felt energized by the activity, the community looked dramatically better after just a few days, in spite of the thousands of destroyed homes in the area. This buoyed the feelings of the children *and* the adults.

Some Cautionary Statements

Some psychosocial support programs conducted by various organizations encourage children to participate in various play activities. This can be very helpful for children in recovering from traumatic events. But it is important not to analyze a child's play. There is very little scientific evidence to indicate what some particular play activity or style "means." However, if a child tends to repeatedly act out their experiences during the traumatic event for an extended period of time, it may be profitable to help the child find a happier way to resolve their dramatic play.

One study involved children who had experienced a flash flood and were reenacting the flood over and over in their play. Parents and teachers were worried about them. The researchers encouraged the children to build a model of their town with large cardboard boxes and to decorate them like buildings in the town. Then they asked the children to be the flood and to show what happened to the town. The children swept through the town crushing the boxes and knocking them aside. Up to this point, the activity was similar in character to what the children had been doing in their play at school and in their homes. But this time, when the "town" of cardboard boxes had been destroyed, the researchers brought in a set of fresh new boxes and asked the children to rebuild their town the way they would like it to be. This simple exercise resulted in a rapid recovery for the children, and followup showed that the children continued to do well long after this intervention.

Similarly, many programs encourage children to draw pictures of their experiences. Again, this may be useful as one option among a number of possible activities for the child's play time. It is important to understand, however, that it is not useful to interpret the child's drawings. There are no data that support interpreting a particular feature of a drawing as indicating that a child is feeling some particular emotion, or of themes in drawings reflecting some specific psychological state. Rather, if a child does choose to draw a picture about the event, it may provide a useful insight to *ask the child to tell you about the drawing*, letting them tell you about their perception of the traumatic event.

It is best to ask the child to tell you about the picture rather than try to interpret it. Photographer: Gerard Jacobs.

Drawing can definitely be overdone as an activity, however. I recall being in Sri Lanka about 9 months after the tsunami had ravaged the area. While consulting in a school, a teacher announced that another non-governmental organization was coming to the school that day. One of the children cried out in the local language. I asked my interpreter what the child said, and he replied, "Oh no! Please don't make us draw again." Many organizations were using the drawings as ways of diagnosing the children's psychological health, a strategy that has no scientific validity.

Finally, let me remind you that it is useful to be aware that parents may also be having difficulty if their child is struggling. If you are providing PFA for a child, make sure to check in with the parents too if you can. Children usually do not recover until after their parents do.

CASE EXAMPLE[1]

Context. More than 87,000 people were killed and 375,000 people were injured as the result of an 8.0 magnitude earthquake that took place in Sichuan province and the surrounding provinces of Gansu and Shaanxi in Western China on May 12, 2008. The quake also caused the initial displacement of up to 15 million people and left more than 5 million homes destroyed. The affected areas continued to experience aftershocks for a long period after the primary quake. The psychological toll of such devastation was high not only among the survivors but for all those living in the region.

Many school buildings were damaged by the tremors and thousands of children died in the collapsed schools. Many students who survived the quake witnessed their classmates dying and had difficulty recovering from their grief.

Psychosocial support has been an integral component of the emergency relief and recovery operations of the Red Cross Society of China in response to this disaster. The psychosocial intervention was continued for 5 years after the disaster and as a result, over 20,000 primary and middle school students and teachers were reached in the most affected province of Sichuan.

Main idea. The psychological support intervention was intended to support children who had survived school collapses and other children enrolled in primary and middle schools in the quake-affected areas. The program also worked with the children's parents and teachers to introduce the concept of community-based psychosocial support (basically our concept of CBPFA) and gain their support. Trained community volunteers worked with the children in classroom settings, usually in teams and, when necessary, with individual students.

Sichuan province is the home of pandas in China and every child from the area has special feelings for panda. So the volunteers introduced a fluffy panda toy named Qiu Qiu (Little Ball in Chinese) to encourage the children to open up and express their inner feelings and loss. The children used Qiu Qiu to tell their stories and this method of storytelling was useful in allowing children to move forward from their pain and grief. Other techniques such as drawing, telling stories, and team games were also used.

The school children spent most of their day in school, so the teachers were taught how to observe and detect early signs that a child required a referral to professional help. The high value that Chinese society places on education means that there is a great deal of pressure on students to succeed in schools. Therefore, it was not surprising that the first and most common sign of emotional distress among the surviving children was poor academic performance. The teachers and parents were encouraged to deal with such situations with a great deal of sensitivity and patience.

[1] This case example was provided by Amgaa Oyungerel, a physician and psychosocial worker in Mongolia with extensive experience in international humanitarian work. The author is very grateful for not only this contribution, but for her service to many affected countries.

PSYCHOLOGICAL SUPPORT FOR CHILDREN WITH DISABILITIES[1]

Two of the most vulnerable groups after a disaster are children and those with disabilities. However, little exists in the literature about the intersection of these two populations: children with disabilities. The U.S. Department of Education indicates approximately 9% of school-age children are involved in special education services. The World Health Organization (2005) estimated that the percentage is significantly higher in developing countries and that 80% of all children with disabilities live in these countries (Peek and Stough, 2010). In 2001, WHO's International Classification of Functioning, Disability, and Health integrated health and disability, conceptualizing disability as occurring from an interaction between an individual's health condition and the individual's personal and environmental setting (WHO, 2001). Furthermore, the likelihood of a disability increases with exposure to disasters, war, and landmine explosions, events that are more common in developing countries. There are several reasons for this increase in the face of disasters. First and foremost is the fact that many children in developing countries live in poverty. With poverty comes lower quality of housing, which places residents at increased risk for damage, loss of possessions, direct exposure, and injury with disasters. Those in poverty also have fewer resources, making evacuation more difficult. Finally, those in poverty have less means to prepare for disasters and are less likely to receive and understand messages related to disasters (Fothergill and Peek, 2004). Issues of evacuation and safety actions are further compromised in children with disabilities. For example, if children have disabilities related to their mobility, then, the ability to go to higher ground to escape floods or to descend stairs to seek shelter in case of storms is significantly compromised. For children with cognitive disabilities, signs related to disasters and dangers may not be fully understood. These children may be more confused and anxious when confronted with emergency signals and actions (Peek & Stough, 2010). All of these factors place children with disabilities at a significant disadvantage in a disaster and at an increased risk for mental health concerns such as posttraumatic stress disorder (Balbus and Malina, 2009; Peek and Stough, 2010; Weissbecker et al., 2008).

Unfortunately, although children with disabilities are an extremely vulnerable population in disasters, they are often absent from emergency preparedness planning (Peek and Stough, 2010). Disaster plans generally assume that children with disabilities will be cared for by their parents. However, disasters often strike when children are at school or other settings removed from their families (Mitchell et al., 2008). When separated, there is an increase in risk for anxiety and stress as well as an increased risk that health-care needs will not be met (Rosenfeld et al., 2010). Children with disabilities may have trouble communicating, making triage more difficult (Baker and Baker, 2010). When this occurs, children with disabilities are at increased risk for secondary illnesses, malnutrition, disease, and abuse (Kinne et al., 2004; Peek and Stough, 2010). Shelters may not be adequately prepared to manage those children with special health-care needs, a concern more likely in developing countries (IOM, 2001) and the children may have difficulty adjusting to life in a shelter (Murray, 2011). If children are with their parents, problems after a disaster remain. Parents may not always have accurate information related to diagnoses, medications, and health-care needs, and health records may not exist in the aftermath of disasters (Baker and Baker, 2010).

A survey by the National Center for Disaster Preparedness reported that approximately 66% of the general population feel unprepared for a disaster (Redlener et al., 2007) and this is higher in families with children with disabilities and special health-care needs (Baker & Baker, 2010). Families reported that, although they are willing to prepare, they do not know what actions to take (Baker & Baker, 2010). To best serve the needs of this most vulnerable population, it is important to incorporate actions and ideas to support these children into disaster planning.

The American Academy of Pediatrics (2015) has recommended special attention to preparation of disaster supply kits for families with children with disabilities. In addition to medications and food for special dietary needs, families need to consider and plan for a power supply for refrigeration of food and medications as well as for medical equipment. Alternate modes of transportation also need to be incorporated into plans. For example, it may be necessary to have a manual wheelchair if an electric wheelchair is unavailable or to have portable ramps/slides to help with mobility issues. All children need special comfort items when distressed. For children with special needs, attention to items that are significant to the child need to have a high priority in disaster planning actions to help soothe distress (eg, toys, music, including batteries to power devices, blankets) (Villaverde, Wong, Gurwitch, & Haydon, 2014). Children with disabilities may be aided by service animals; planning for care of these animals is also important (Gurwitch, 2014). Family emergency plans will benefit from proactive steps. These include educating children with disabilities about actions to take in case of emergency (use of visual schedules may help) and reviewing these on a regular basis (Shore, 2006; Gurwitch and Newgass, 2009).

Because children with special needs may be in schools when disasters strike, planning for response and recovery within the educational system is important. Approximately one-quarter of schools in the United States have no disaster provisions for children with disabilities (Graham et al., 2006). The International Federation of Red Cross and Red Crescent Societies (2007) noted that children with disabilities often have a harder time accessing educational services *without* the presence of a disaster. When a disaster strikes, their access to services and special needs (eg, ramps) are given a lower priority during recovery efforts. Teachers are an important support for children with special needs after a disaster. Yet few receive appropriate training for understanding and helping these students after disasters (Ducy and Stough, 2011). The Autism Society of America (Shore, 2006) recommended that first responders also have special training and information related to helping children with disabilities in times of disaster. In addition to visual alerts about the presence of a child with special needs in the home, the society recommended educating first responders about how to engage and support these children. For example, children with autism may not fully understand or be able to respond to those coming to help, making rescue efforts more difficult.

Effective communication is critical after a disaster to assure appropriate actions are taken. Many of the messaging and communication principles that apply to children without disabilities can be amended to apply to those with special needs. For example, it is important to speak in a way that children with disabilities will understand. To increase likelihood of clear communications, adults need to avoid abstract language such as using "gone" to describe someone deceased, and use "died" instead. Explanations need to be tailored to match a child's developmental level (Murray, 2011). In fact, children with autism and other disabilities may also not fully understand death and be confused by changes due to the loss (Gurwitch and Newgass, 2009). Multiple ways to allow expression and understanding are also important; these include pictures (particularly of recovery and support actions), drawing materials, and emotion faces (Moseley et al., 2007). Repetition is important for children with disabilities. Therefore, adults' patience is needed to answer and reanswer questions, provide on-going information several times, and to recheck children's understanding of what is happening and what is being done to protect and care for them (Gurwitch and Newgass, 2009). Children in general, and children with cognitive disabilities in particular, may not fully understand media coverage of disaster-related events. To reduce distress and risk for mental health concerns, it is best to limit a child's media exposure (Gurwitch et al., 2002; Moseley et al., 2007).

In sum, children with disabilities are a uniquely vulnerable population after a disaster. Preparedness planning related to children with disabilities, including specialized training for those responding to as well as for those supporting these children need to be included for communities, schools, and families. Finally, research to better understand the issues of this population is essential to assure best practices can be developed in disaster response. By increasing our understanding of the special needs of children with disabilities, the health and mental health outcomes for these children can be improved.

[1] This information on children with disabilities is provided by Dr. Robin Gurwitch. She is a noted authority on psychological support for children. She is a faculty member and PCIT-International Master Trainer at Duke University Medical Center and Center Child and Family Health, which is a consortium of Duke University, North Carolina Central University, and University of North Carolina at Chapel Hill.

References

American Academy of Pediatrics, 2015. Children and youth with special needs. Available from: www.aap.org.

Baker, L. R., & Baker, M. D. (2010). Disaster preparedness among families of children with special health care needs. *Disaster Med. Public Health Prep.*, *4*, 240–245.

Balbus, J. M., & Malina, A. B. (2009). Identifying vulnerable subpopulations for climate change health effects in the United States. *Int. J. Occup. Environ. Med.*, *51*, 33–37.

Ducy, E. M., & Stough, L. M. (2011). Exploring the support role of special education teachers after Hurricane Ike: children with significant disabilities. *J. Fam. Issues, 32*, 1325–1345.

Fothergill, A., & Peek, L. (2004). Poverty and disasters in the United States: a review of the sociological literature. *Nat. Hazards, 32*, 89–110.

Graham, J., Shirm, S., Liggin, R., Aiken, M. E., & Dick, R. (2006). Mass-casualty events at schools: a national preparedness survey. *Pediatrics, 117,* e8–e15.

Gurwitch, R.H., 2014. Children and disaster behavioral health response. Workshop for the Center for Multicultural Mental Health, Boston Medical Center, and the Emergency Preparedness Bureau (MA Department of Mental Health), Springfield, MA.

Gurwitch, R.H., Newgass, S., 2009. Atypical needs in crises: autism and unique considerations. Autism Spectrum Quarterly, May.

Gurwitch, R. H., Sitterle, K. S., Young, B. H., & Pfefferbaum, B. (2002). The aftermath of terrorism. In A. LaGreca, W. Silverman, E. Vernberg, & M. Roberts (Eds.), *Helping Children Cope With Disasters and Terrorism* (pp. 327–357). Washington, DC: American Psychological Association Press.

Institute of Medicine (2001). *Neurological, Psychiatric, and Developmental Disorders: Meeting the Challenge in the Developing World.* Washington, DC: National Academy Press.

International Federation of Red Cross and Red Crescent Societies. (2007). *World Disasters Report: 2007 Focus on Discrimination.* Bloomfield, CT: Kumarian Press.

Kinne, S., Patrick, D. L., & Doyle, D. L. (2004). Prevalence of secondary conditions among people with disabilities. *Am. J. Public Health, 94,* 443–445.

Mitchell, T., Haynes, K., Hall, N., Choong, W., & Oven, K. (2008). The role of children and youth in communicating disaster risk. *Children Youth Environ., 18,* 254–279.

Moseley, C., Salmi, P., Johnstone, C., and Gaylord, V. (Eds.), 2007. Impact: Feature Issue on Disaster Preparedness and People With Disabilities. University of Minnesota, Institute on Community Integration, Minneapolis, p. 20.

Murray, J. S. (2011). Disaster preparedness for children with special healthcare needs and disabilities. *J. Spec. Pediatr. Nurs., 16,* 226–232.

Peek, L., & Stough, L. M. (2010). Children with disabilities in the context of disaster: a social vulnerability perspective. *Child Dev., 81,* 1260–1270.

Redlener, I., Abramson, D., Stehling-Ariza, T., Grant, R., and Johnson, D., 2007. The American preparedness project: Where the U.S. public stands in 2007 on terrorism, security, and disaster preparedness. Survey by the National Center for Disaster Preparedness. Columbia University Mailman School of Public Health and The Children's Health Fund. Available from: http://www.ncdp.mailman.columbia.edu/files/NCDP07.pdf

Rosenfeld, L. B., Caye, J. S., Lahad, M., & Gurwitch, R. H. (2010). *When Their World Falls Apart: Helping Families and Children Manage the Effects of Disasters.* Washington, DC: NASW Press.

Shore, S.M., 2006. Disaster preparedness for people on the Autism Spectrum [and all individuals with disabilities] and their supporters. One hour training retrieved from *www.autism.com.*

Villaverde, V., Wong, M., Gurwitch, R., Haydon, S., 2014. Understanding and Supporting Students in Times of Crisis: A Disaster Framework for Communities and Schools. Training provided for the Republic of the Philippines Department of Education, Tagatay and Cebu, Republic of the Philippines.

Weissbecker, I., Sephton, S., Martin, M., & Simpson, D. (2008). Psychological and physiological correlates of stress in children exposed to disaster: review of current research and recommendations for intervention. *Children Youth Environ., 18,* 30–70.

World Health Organization. (2001). *International Classification of Functioning, Disability, and Health.* Geneva, Switzerland: Author.

World Health Organization. (2005). *Disability, Including Prevention, Management, and Rehabilitiation.* Geneva, Switzerland: World Health Organization.

15

OLDER ADULTS AND PEOPLE WITH DISABILITIES

L.M. Brown

Palo Alto University, Palo Alto, CA, United States

CHAPTER OUTLINE

Many people assume that disability naturally occurs with increasing age. However, people of all ages can and do have disabilities. Age alone does not increase vulnerability. As a community responder it is likely that you will encounter a number of children, adolescents, and adults of all ages who have sensory (eg, vision or hearing problems), physical, or mental impairment. Some disabilities may be easy to see while others may be less evident. Responders should be mindful of the wide range of strengths, needs, and issues for people with disabilities. In some instances, delivery of psychological first aid interventions may need to be modified because no single approach works for everyone. Rather than guessing about how you should offer assistance and what type might be most beneficial, your best option is to simply ask how you can help. It is safe to assume that physical appearance of advanced age does not equate with disability or incapacity to respond or recover from disasters. In fact, many older people can assist others by serving as volunteers or paid staff.

For people of all ages, poverty, low education, limited social networks, and isolation play a role in shaping overall vulnerability. In general, people who depend on others for assistance with activities of daily living are at greater risk for poor outcomes after disasters. Not surprisingly, disasters place a severe strain on both personal well-being and social support networks. Who is at risk will differ as a function of circumstances. For example, a physically healthy, community-dwelling, 70-year old person with a large and active social network is vulnerable during a disaster, along with the rest of the general public, but a frail, socially isolated, home-bound older adult of the same age may be extremely vulnerable. Relatively recent health care advances have improved the overall physical and mental functioning of many younger people and as a result successive generations are demonstrating health levels that are comparable to that of younger adults from earlier cohorts. It is useful to know that it is not age per se, but the presence of a constellation of factors such as: sensory, mobility, and cognitive impairment; physical decline; and medical illness that increases risk for adverse outcomes during and after disasters. Physical, cognitive (ie, ability to think), and sensory impairments that hinder functioning may limit access to services and material goods, such as food and water, from disaster assistance centers. Although the discussion in this chapter is focused primarily on use of CBPFA with older adults, the types of accommodations that might be helpful for adults of any age who have a disability can be found at the end of this chapter.

Development Issues and Individual Risk Factors in Late Life

Older adulthood is a developmental stage at the end of the lifespan. It is a time when people experience changes in physical appearance and body composition. Aging is a dynamic and highly individualized process. Because of variability in this age group, it is difficult to generalize and make blanket statements that apply to everyone in late life. As you recall the example of the two different 70-year old people described previously, consider that most disaster educational materials and psychological first aid training programs classify all people who are 65 years and older as a vulnerable population. Just as there are considerable differences between a 1-year old and a 10-year old, the same is true for older adults. In the United States, all people who are 18 years and older are considered adults. A further distinction is made between young-adults, middle-aged adults, and older adults. However, just as it does not make sense to lump all ages of children together because of their developmental differences, it is useful to distinguish between those who are young-old (65–74 years of age), old-old (75–84 years of age), and oldest-old (85 years and older).

Age-related changes can increase vulnerability to both acute and chronic physical illness as well as mark the onset of functional limitations such as decreased mobility, poor vision, or diminished hearing ability. If you have older persons in your family or as friends or neighbors, of if you want to provide support in the broader community, understanding developmental issues in late life is not only helpful, but necessary. Because older adults are the fastest growing age group in the United States, it is likely that after a disaster you will encounter many people who are 65 years of age and older. Notably, this subgroup is also becoming increasingly racially and ethnically diverse. As noted previously, not all 70-year-olds are alike. Some may play a vital role during the recovery process from a disaster or other traumatic event, while others may need ongoing assistance. Again, the best way to quickly determine who needs help and how that help might best be provided is to simply ask the person.

What is Normal Aging?

As people age, most maintain their everyday intelligence, learning potential, and language ability while developing wisdom and emotional intelligence. In addition, a majority of older adults report a sense of well-being and good mood despite encountering loss and experiencing physical decline. However, it is not unusual for older adults to require additional time for problem solving and to demonstrate slower word retrieval and processing speed. If you have ever experienced a moment when you could not quickly recall the name of a song, or perhaps you have walked into a room but then could not remember what you planned to retrieve there, those moments, where the information pops into your head a few minutes later become more common in late life. The information is there but it is harder to freely recall when under stress or time pressure. It takes more time to think and respond. In late old age (85 years and older), people generally experience physical and mental changes, and in very late old age, these declines are almost universal.

Older couple at opening of McDonald's in Moscow. Photographer: Jean-Pierre Revel.

Although age-related physical changes do not necessarily result in disease, most of the older adults have at least one chronic health condition such as arthritis, chronic obstructive pulmonary disease, diabetes, or osteoporosis. The growing number of older people who are likely to have one or more chronic health conditions effectively increases the pool of vulnerable people who may be at greater risk for problems after a disaster and who may need more psychological support. Moreover, because more people are able to live independently in the community with one or more chronic health conditions, some people do not self-identify as having a limitation that would require them to need assistance after a disaster. It is only when electrical power is unavailable to recharge an electric scooter or when a home health aide is unable to make a scheduled visit, that the disability becomes apparent and potentially harmful. In such situations psychological support for older family, friends, and neighbors becomes very important. In Florida, after a major hurricane, there were numerous reports of older people who became trapped in their high-rise apartments when the electrical power went off. Emergency responders had to carry people down several flights of stairs to evacuate them to safe shelters.

Older people typically experience numerous losses and stressors, such as fixed income and increasing expenses; deaths or relocation of relatives, neighbors, and friends; decreasing social network; changes in social position and housing; and spousal death or caregiving responsibilities. Although some older adults may have poorer health and fewer social and economic resources compared to younger adults, they have a lifetime of experience in coping with stressful events. Being able to think back to an earlier time and identify an event where they were able to successfully deal with a major stressor often provides confidence and perspective about their ability to recover from the current situation. If you use the SODA problem-solving model discussed in Chapter 7, those prior successful strategies will come up in asking about coping strategies used in the past.

Not surprisingly, there are adults in all age groups for whom health problems and mental disorders exacerbate life's challenges. Exposure to traumatic events, such as disasters, represents a unique stressor that has its impact within the context of a person's preexisting functioning. Given that some disorders (eg, dementia, delirium) are increasingly likely with age, it is useful to possess a basic understanding of each these conditions as well as fundamental knowledge of older adults' reactions to traumatic stressors.

Older Adults' Reactions to Traumatic Stress

Traumatic stress reactions may present differently in older adults. Developmental factors (eg, maturity, perspective, reduced future in which recovery can take place) can increase resilience *OR* vulnerability depending on the context in which the traumatic event occurred and the types of supports available after the event. Many people experience more than one traumatic event in the course of a lifetime. Thus, consideration of the impact of traumatic stress on older adults needs to take into account both the cumulative effect of traumatic stress exposure across the lifespan and the possibility that traumatic experiences may have different effects depending on when they occur during the life course. For example, a fire that destroys a home and a person's possessions may be experienced differently by a 22-year-old starting out in life with few belongings, a large social network, but low financial resources compared to a 72-year-old who has lost five decades worth of acquired mementos and keepsakes, has a dwindling social network, but has substantial savings and insurance.

An older adult's response to traumatic stress depends on culture, personality, preexisting physical and mental health, social support, availability of resources, and hidden stressors. A hidden stressor is a traumatic experience that was experienced in early life but not adequately resolved and now compounds or worsens the reaction to the current stressor. The current stressor is thought to trigger buried earlier stressor memories that may not until now have been problematic in regard to day-to-day functioning. Remembering that older people have a past that is filled with both positive and negative events is wise. An unusually strong reaction to the current stressor may in fact be influenced by past events. When presented with this additional historical context, it is not unusual for providers of CBPFA to normalize the strong response to the current traumatic event. It is understandable to think, "I would be upset too if that had happened to me. This is a normal response given all that has occurred to this person. This person does not need any special assistance because their reaction is understandable." Even if it seems reasonable that the past event is adversely affecting current functioning, it does not mean that the person would not benefit from CBPFA or follow-up care if needed.

Many older people express their psychological reaction to a traumatic stressor with physical complaints. They are more likely to want to see a primary care physician for help with sleeping or appetite problems, than to seek out psychological intervention to treat the underlying anxiety or depression. In part, this may be due to the stigma of using mental health services or cultural differences in expression of psychological problems. Moreover, older adults without previous experience with the mental health system may not understand what crisis counseling can or cannot do to help with recovery postdisaster. These are some of the reasons that a friend or neighbor may be an effective provider of psychological support through CBPFA.

Response to traumatic stressors is not limited to emotional, or physical reactions, but also includes memory, relationships, and behavior change. Memory or concentration problems resulting from the traumatic experience can affect an older person's ability to make sense of traumatic memories and integrate sensory information. The processing of traumatic memories depends on insight, maturity, and subjective understanding of the traumatic event. CBPFA plays a role in helping people cope and use adaptive strategies to deal with the current situation and to potentially minimize future psychological problems. However, people with cognitive impairment resulting from dementia or delirium may have unique challenges in coping with difficult times.

Delirium

Delirium presents as a sudden change in mental function and is considered a medical emergency. Older adults with delirium usually fade in and out of consciousness, have difficulty paying attention, are disoriented, and sometimes are delusional. A delusion is an idea that does not make sense, but is unshakable. The person's speech may be disjointed and nonsensical. Causes of delirium are diverse and include heat stroke, drug interactions, urinary tract infections, failure to adequately manage diabetes, and uncontrolled pain. Older adults are highly susceptible to delirium when their health care is compromised or disrupted. Although delirium is treatable—and associated with increased risk of morbidity and mortality if untreated—it often goes unrecognized, especially in older adults where the symptoms may be misinterpreted as part of an ongoing dementia. Older adults who do not have a friend, neighbor, or familiar caregiver to advocate for them and identify the sudden onset of cognitive and behavioral changes may be at particular risk of failing to receive appropriate and timely medical attention. If you encounter a person who appears to be confused, it is best to refer them to a medical provider or mental health professional who can assess for the presence of delirium or dementia and make appropriate referrals.

Dementia

Dementia is a progressively debilitating neurological syndrome. It is associated with a progressive loss of memory and other intellectual functions that interfere with the ability of the person to function independently and perform self-care activities. It represents a decline from previous level of functioning. Although there are many diseases that result in dementia, the most common is Alzheimer's disease. Alzheimer's disease is a progressive, irreversible disease characterized by memory loss and problems learning new information. If you are providing psychological support to someone you do not know, it is likely to be difficult to determine if the current level of functioning is life-long or more recent in onset. However, this determination does not have to be made by you. Similar to the cautions taken with delirium, if a person appears confused, family members, neighbors, or friends who know and are familiar with the older adult would best be consulted to see if the current level of functioning is significantly different from the recent past. If the change is recent or sudden, the older adult needs to be referred for further evaluation by a professional. Under the best conditions, health care providers often find it difficult to discern between delirium and dementia in patients where previous level of functioning is unknown. After a disaster, these diagnostic challenges increase because people living in public shelters or in community settings are often strangers and the environment can be loud, chaotic, and confusing. Referral to a medical or mental health professional is not only useful, it helps keep the person with impaired functioning safe during a difficult time.

There is a large literature on dementia care that documents the importance of a supportive physical and social environment to maintain the delicate equilibrium of older adults with dementia.

Much is known about how to avoid escalation of problem behaviors, emotional distress, and cognitive deterioration through consistent, responsive care provided by familiar caregivers who are versed in the strategies and nuances of dementia care. Unfortunately, the unpredictability and chaos associated with disasters is the opposite of a calm and supportive environment. In some areas, special needs shelters may be available to accommodate this vulnerable subgroup of the population.

Emotions

Depression and anxiety are emotions that are often experienced after a traumatic event. Although feeling anxious is an extremely common reaction to a traumatic stressor, the presence of this feeling is more likely to result in avoidance behaviors than in actions to obtain psychological support. As you might expect after reading about the benefits of social networks, avoidance behaviors are generally not a good way to adjust after a disaster.

Another age-related concept that may be particularly important for responders to understand is that older people may have a different perception of the relative value of both symbolic and material losses. Material losses can extend beyond personal keepsakes and include neighborhood trees, a favorite coffee shop, or other environmental markers that will not be reestablished during the course of their lifetime. Others may grieve that the United States is no longer safe from terrorist attacks or crime. Responders should avoid minimizing end of life issues. The older one is, the more compressed one's timeline is for recovery, often with a reduced set of social and material resources. The cumulative physical, cognitive, social and financial losses can progressively deplete an older adults' capacity for resilience. People may feel depressed and anxious when dealing with these changes and losses. It is tempting to think that it is normal to feel depressed in response to losses of this magnitude and that it is not necessary for follow-up care. Feelings of depression that adversely affect daily functioning should not be ignored in adults of any age. In instances where intervention with CBPFA appears inadequate, refer the person to a mental health or medical professional.

However, it is interesting to note that many older adults reported positive as well as negative outcomes to disaster experiences. After the 2004 hurricanes in Florida, I interviewed older adults about their disaster experiences. Some explained that they were saddened by the loss of close neighbors who had decided to move after the storm. Social groups, such as bridge clubs and senior centers, as well as religious organizations lost participants in the days and weeks after the storm. The older adults who remained in the area reported distress resulting from the damage to their community that was then followed by additional losses to their social network. However, it was not all doom and gloom. In contrast, others reported that they felt closer to God, had improved relations with neighbors, and had a new personal and meaningful tie to their community as a survivor. One older woman explained that when the electrical power went off during the storm, all the food in her freezer, as well as that of her neighbors, had to be cooked or disposed of as it defrosted in the following days. She described a scene where neighbors who had not previously had much contact with each other were now cooking their food together on outside grills and sharing meals. She said that her relationship with her neighbors had changed for the better and that she was very grateful she no longer felt so alone.

It is important to remember that sources of resilience and risk factors for disproportionate vulnerability will vary within the population of older adults. Responders should consider that healthy older adults are essentially similar to the general population in terms of needs and resources. Community dwelling older adults with functional needs will require assistance in preparing and recovering, and frail, institutionalized older adults with very limited functional ability will depend heavily on the existing health care systems to remain secure and safe.

Special Needs Shelters Following Disasters and Use of Services

During evacuation, older adults sustain more injuries than any other age group due to fragile muscles, impaired balance, low endurance, and susceptibility to hypothermia, hyperthermia, and dehydration. Even once safely moved to a public shelter, the presence of disability and preexisting health conditions need to be taken into consideration. In shelters with significant background noise and chaos, auditory, visual, and cognitive deficits can all hinder an older person's ability to understand and act on directions for obtaining food, water, and other vital necessities. Even for those who use hearing aids and eyeglasses, it is not uncommon for batteries to no longer function or for reading glasses to be lost during an evacuation. Cognitive impairments (ie, problems with thinking and memory) can result in disorientation and confusion in an unfamiliar environment.

Although special needs shelters are designed to accommodate those who need extra support to maintain health and functioning during and after disasters, many people do not preregister for this service because they do not consider themselves as having special needs or grasp the potential benefit from using this service. Registration requirements for special needs shelter vary by state and county. Typically, written verification by a physician and documentation that a family or friend is unable to assist with shelter or transportation during a disaster is required to qualify for these services. Therefore, if you have family, friends, or neighbors who are older who may need extra assistance, it may be profitable to help them obtain such verification in preparation for possible disasters. This would be an additional step in the preparation for instrumental assistance described in Chapter 9.

This mismatch, between how disaster services are explained or marketed to older people and their actual use by those for whom they are intended, continues today. The end result is that shelter planners are unable to fully plan for the total number of unregistered people who may show-up requesting services at a special needs shelter. Other people who would benefit from special needs shelters end up at public shelters that lack the equipment and staff needed to assist with their activities of daily living. Public shelters are usually noisy, crowded, and lack privacy. The environment in public shelters is stressful and can present obstacles to care. Older adults may feel unsafe, overwhelmed, and unable to advocate for their needs. If you wind up staying in a shelter as a resident or as a volunteer, it would be profitable to take particular note of the possible need for support of older residents.

If an older adult you are supporting needs to move to a public shelter, it is optimal to accompany them because they may require more assistance than what is available postevent. Although you might expect first responders to be knowledgeable about the needs of older adults, information about aging issues (eg, potential risk factors, strengths, common health problems) is often not included in standard psychological first aid training. Although it is increasingly important for public health and disaster relief workers to learn about issues specific to older adults as well as to be educated about stereotypes and myths, the content covered in most psychological first aid training programs is inadequate. As a CBPFA provider, you may possess more practical knowledge about aging issues from having read this chapter than many professional relief workers do even after having completed multiple trainings.

Social Networks and Caregiving Issues

Many older adults have supportive friends, neighbors, and relatives, although their immediate family may not necessarily live in the same community. Due to a combination of circumstances and choices, some older adults are at significant risk for social isolation. People who are likely to have few interpersonal relationships or social roles are those who are very old (85 years of age and older), have a difficult time moving independently, have limited finances, or have poor health. Social factors that increase likelihood of social isolation include changes in family structure, a highly mobile society, and trends that discourage communal living arrangements for older adults in favor of independent residency.

Having a discussion with an older adult can be rewarding for both participants.
Photographer: Gerard Jacobs.

Informal caregivers, such as relatives, neighbors, and friends, often play a key role in helping older adults. The number of people in the older adults' social network, along with the degree of closeness and level of activity, has the potential to buffer many of the negative effects of stressors and promote better mental health functioning. After a disaster, preexisting social networks are often the first line of defense by providing practical assistance such as obtaining safe shelter, food, water, and health care. The belief that others care about you and will provide assistance if needed, results in better psychological outcomes following a disaster.

However, social networks are also vulnerable to disruption and decline after a disaster because many informal caregivers will also be survivors of the same event. Caregiver assistance is less available when property is damaged or destroyed, electricity or phone communication are not functioning, or daily routines are disrupted. Additionally, informal caregivers may be unable to assist because their current needs exceed their available resources.

Many middle-aged adults have responsibilities for providing care to their children and parents as well as working outside the home. These types of challenges, coupled with activities to recover from a disaster, can be a heavy burden. It is easy to understand why informal caregivers are often encouraged to arrange for emergency respite care in advance of a disaster for older adult family members with significant supervision and care needs. Because of their advanced age, most of the older adults are unlikely to shoulder this type of responsibility except those who are primary caregivers for their grandchildren.

Compounding the situation, deterioration of the local infrastructure decreases the availability of assistance through community-based services, religious, and nonprofit organizations. As a result, the need for support and services for disaster survivors of all ages may surpass availability of existing resources. In the ensuing shortage, the needs of many older adults are likely to go unmet. Aspects of the social and physical environment can worsen or lessen stress, particularly for the most vulnerable segment of the older adult population—those who are frail or cognitively impaired. While social networks are disrupted and depleted, CBPFA can provide much needed support and assistance.

Strategies for Supporting Older Adults

In some instances, CBPFA may have to be modified to accommodate health and mental health issues. For example, older adults with impaired hearing may benefit from encouragement to use their hearing aids or, if available, use of a portable amplifying device. Speaking clearly while facing the person will also aid in reading lips and detecting facial expressions. Not all older adults may admit to needing hearing aids or reading glasses as assistive devices.

Older adults with vision problems who need corrective lenses to read print material may not be able to complete forms to obtain aid if they have misplaced their reading glasses. Some older adults may sign documents without being able to adequately see them or fully understand their content. The older a person is, the more likely they are to have low literacy. Some older adults are ashamed that they are poor readers or unable to read and may not readily disclose their difficulties. Standard print materials should be available in alternative formats such as large print, Braille, and audio recordings. Because of poor disaster literacy, it is often beneficial to repeat and deliver information through multiple media.

If you have concerns about a person's ability to follow directions and function independently, that person should not be left alone for safety reasons. Although it may not be clear if a person should be referred for more formal follow-up, assessing for orientation is a low tech and quick method for making that decision. A series of questions to assess orientation to time, place, person, and event can be asked to detect presence of impairment and need for additional evaluation. If a person is struggling or confused about orientation questions, he or she may have more serious issues that require evaluation and treatment. Following is an example of how orientation questions could be asked.

CBPFA provider: "What's your name?"

Older adult: "Julia."

CBPFA provider: "Do you know where you are Julia?"

Older adult: "I'm in a public shelter."

CBPFA provider: "Do you know what day and time it is?"

Older adult: "I think it's Wednesday morning" (the correct response).

CBPFA provider: "Do you know why you are here?"

Older adult: "Yes. A tornado damaged my home. I am here until I have a safe place to live" (the correct response).

Although noted previously, I want to again emphasize that people without a known, preexisting cognitive impairment who are not thinking clearly in the aftermath of a disaster should be further evaluated to rule out the presence of medical illness, heat stroke, dehydration, delirium, drug mismanagement, and other conditions that may require immediate medical treatment. In general, older adults are confronted with greater challenges under adverse circumstances than are younger adults. Following is a case example that highlights some of the concerns you will want to address when working with an older adult after a disaster.

TRY THIS

Jose is an 84-year-old grandfather. His wife died several years before a hurricane struck his small town in the south of Florida. His daughter was forced to evacuate to another community and was unable to provide Jose with assistance and support before or after the storm. It appears that it will take several days until the roads are cleared and electricity and phone service are restored. He is living at home although there is some structural damage by floods and wind. Jose owns a small dog and is not willing to move into a local shelter because he fears that his home will be looted if left unoccupied and is unwilling to be separated from his pet. He appears sad and isolated. He has his meals delivered by a concerned neighbor, but is running low on dog food.

What are your main concerns with Jose? How could you use psychological first aid techniques to help him? Jose just informed you about the details of the hurricane. How do you respond?

Start by allowing adequate time to talk with Jose and establish rapport as you listen, answer questions, and provide information. The goal is not for Jose to disclose any or all of the details concerning his hurricane experience, but rather to restore a sense of safety and control by promoting use of adaptive coping skills and helping him remain as functionally independent as possible. Is English Jose's primary language? Is he able to understand the information you are providing and if not, how could you tailor your message so that he could better understand what you are trying to communicate? If Jose has a sensory impairment or disability that could potentially affect his safety, ask him what types of assistance would be most helpful. Determine if Jose is safe, but respect his choices and promote self-efficacy and independence by working as a partner to address his disaster-related problems and enhance his coping abilities. Check to see if he has been in contact with his daughter since the storm. If phone services are operable, offer Jose an opportunity to call his daughter to encourage reestablishing contact with his informal and formal social network. Check to see what types of resources are available for his dog. Does his neighbor have extra dog food that they might be able to share? Explore the types of assistance his neighbors might be able to offer until services are restored and his daughter is able to return to the area. Provide information about available resources. If appropriate, develop a plan for when and how Jose will access needed services.

Disability

The ability to physically or cognitively function is a useful way to understand disability. Function is often divided into two broad categories: *activities of daily living* and *instrumental activities of daily living*. The simpler and more fundamental of these two categories is *activities of daily living* that includes basic living activities such as bathing, dressing, walking, eating, and using the bathroom independently. In contrast, performing *instrumental activities of daily living* requires a higher level of cognitive and physical ability to carry out tasks such as independently managing finances, shopping, preparing meals, cleaning, managing transportation, keeping a schedule, using a telephone, and self-administering medications. When people are not able to independently perform one or more of these activities of daily living, they have some type of disability.

Ability to perform both types of activities of daily living after a disaster is needed to remain safe, maintain function, and engage in activities to facilitate recovery. As noted earlier, under normal daily living conditions, many people with disability can function with minimal assistance or with adaptive technology. If assistance is not available or loss of electricity makes power-operated assistive devices (eg, electric scooters) inoperable, people with disability may become vulnerable and at increased risk for adverse outcomes.

Familiarity with one's home and neighborhood promotes confidence and facilitates ability to optimally function in a known environment. After a disaster, ability to navigate around new hazards and function in a complex and evolving environment may be compromised. When considering how to offer assistance to someone who may be disabled, it is best to ask how help should be provided. Often, people with disabilities have received skill training on how to explain their impairment to others and to be proactive in describing the assistance they would like to receive. In other instances, a medical alert tag or bracelet may prove helpful in providing information. It may be difficult to discern by appearance alone whether a person is disabled and needs assistance. Just as not all older adults are alike, there are differences within each type of disability such as time of onset (eg, birth or late life), speed of onset (eg, gradual or rapid) degree (eg, mild or total deafness), and impact of their disability on functioning over the course of their life.

Consider the possible differences between a child who was born with congenital blindness as opposed to an adult who loses vision later in life due to accident or disease. A person who was born with limited vision is more likely to have learned to read Braille and use a mobility cane in contrast to an older adult who has lost sight from glaucoma or macular degeneration. Adults who lose sight in late life also need to acquire adaptive skills. However, the methods for teaching and the ability to learn new compensatory strategies vary because people born with sight have visual experiences to draw upon and most likely experience their late life vision impairment as a traumatic loss. Following is an overview of issues that should be considered and approaches that might be used to address identified concerns when helping with people with disabilities.

Physical Impairment

Sometimes accommodating people with disabilities requires modifications to the physical environment, such as portable ramps for wheelchair or walkers. However, these accommodations may be damaged or not readily available after a disaster. Makeshift adaptions may be necessary (eg, using a sheet of plywood as a ramp) to move people from unsafe areas. After the Florida hurricanes, there were numerous reports of people with mobility impairment who lived in high-rise buildings having to be carried down flights of stairs when the elevator became damaged or when the power went off for an extended period of time. When possible, people with disabilities should not be separated from adaptive equipment and members of their social support network, such as relatives, friends, aides, and service animals. CBPFA providers can serve as an advocate if a shelter worker says that no animals are allowed in a shelter. Service animals are specifically allowed in American Red Cross shelters. Service animals may also be covered by state or local laws exempting them from other animal restrictions. Learning about your state's laws can be a good activity in preparation for providing instrumental assistance. Separations from critical supports can increase vulnerability and response to traumatic stressors. For some people with disabilities, acute injuries, dangerous evacuations, unfamiliar surroundings, and altered routines serve as triggers for a variety of adverse physical and mental health outcomes that in some instances can result in hospitalization or hasten death.

Visual Impairment

Visual impairment ranges from people with vision problems that can be corrected with eyeglasses to people who have no ability to see light or shapes. As people age, diseases that impair vision become more common. Glaucoma, cataracts, macular degeneration, and diabetic retinopathy are just a few conditions that can make it difficult for people to see as well as increase their risk for falling. If you want to offer help, identify yourself and ask if assistance is desired. If so, invite the person to grip your arm and follow you rather than gripping their arm and pulling them forward.

If you encounter steps or hazards, such as pools of water, uneven or pitted pavement, or debris littering the ground, describe the number of steps or the size and type of obstacle before it is encountered. Let the person know where you are and give an estimate of how long it will take to walk to the intended location. When entering an unfamiliar room, provide a point of reference by walking the person to their seat or placing their hand on the back of the chair, table, or wall.

Hearing Impairment

In public shelters or in large groups of people, hearing high frequency sounds and detecting changes in speech and tone may be difficult for people with hearing impairment. Even people wearing working hearing aids may have difficulty hearing. A mild hearing impairment can result in missed information and reduce ability to interact with others as well as obtain services and secure assistance. Both the speaker sending the message and the listener receiving the message need to work together to successfully communicate. This is likely to require additional energy and patience in the BESTT EARS process.

If you perceive that a person has difficulty hearing, ask how you can best communicate with the person. The person may indicate a preference for receiving information by written word or listening with one ear over the other ear. If hearing is better in one ear, move to that side of the person and touch their hand or arm to capture their attention and indicate you are planning to speak. Maintaining eye contact, facing the listener directly, and keeping your hands away from your face and mouth makes it easier to read facial expressions and see visual cues.

Lip-reading ability is enhanced if you are sitting in good light and not distorting your face by shouting, chewing gum, eating food, speaking rapidly, or over-enunciating. Lips covered by beards and moustaches are problematic because facial hair masks lips and makes it challenging to discern what the speaker is saying. Speak naturally, keep sentences short and simple, and rephrase rather than repeat information that was not understood the first time. Repeated information is unlikely to be understood the second time it is spoken. A better strategy is to rephrase the information or present it in a written format. To confirm the listener knows what was said, ask them to repeat key details and the specifics of the discussion.

Taste, Smell, and Touch Impairments

The impact of taste, smell, and touch is often not considered during or after a disaster. Like other disabilities, some people are born with a poor sense of taste, smell, or touch. In general, women of all ages are better able to detect odors then men, but ability to smell declines after the age of 60, making it more difficult for all older adults to smell smoke or noxious fumes, such as a leaking gas line, that may threaten health and safety. Providing visual and auditory warnings that alert people of a gas leak, are two possible ways to help people evacuate from areas under threat.

Inability to smell and taste may place people at risk for eating food that has spoiled or drinking water that appears clean but smells odd. Chlorine is often added to questionable water, but could be ingested prior to being diluted and drinkable. People with dietary restrictions (eg, food allergies, low-salt diets) may find that the food available after a disaster is not consumable. Food allergy triggers can be difficult to avoid, particularly if the allergen is an ingredient in a meal or mislabeled in an ingredient list. Many people have peanut-triggered life-threatening allergic reactions. The intensity of the reaction depends on the person's age, amount eaten, and if the nuts were cooked or processed. Because an epinephrine injection using an EpiPen can be a life-saving treatment, people should be encouraged to carry a pen with them after a disaster.

People who are not able to use touch to discriminate between hot and cold surfaces, feel pain, or discern the presence of vibration or pressure, may encounter challenges after a disaster. Some people may be unable to detect changes in the surface of the ground under their feet. Although some people are born with impaired touch, many others develop it in late life as a result of type 2 diabetes, arthritis, nerve damage, or head injury. People can experience pain, tingling, numbness or weakness from these and other medical conditions. If you have ever had your foot fall asleep, you have experienced the sensation of pins and needles or a tingling sensation that you most likely experienced as unpleasant. People who routinely experience this sensation as a result of disease or accident, usually have problems with coordination or balance when walking. Check to see if the person would like assistance when walking or what other actions might be taken to help with safety and comfort.

TRY THIS

Although most people will not need more than psychological first aid after a disaster, a select few will benefit from free crisis counseling services and many more will need to access some type of services postdisaster. These services might include obtaining shelter, securing insurance benefits, and receiving medical care. To better understand how challenging it might be for a person with a disability to use services where you live, I ask my students to use the internet or a telephone book to identify all the mental health services that are available within a 20 mile radius from their home (eg, mental health care, substance abuse programs, integrated primary care). Next, I have them determine whether public transportation is available from their home to two different categories of mental health services. Finally, I ask them to estimate how long it would take for them to walk from their home to the bus or train. They are asked to note the cost, availability, comfort, and safety of existing public transportation services. If public transportation is not available, I ask my students to develop a list of ideas for enhancing access to all types of services postdisaster. My students are usually surprised by the limited number of mental health services in their area as well as the cost in time and money to use postdisaster services.

Conclusions

Some older adults and people with disabilities may require greater attention and patience in providing CBPFA, both for general psychological support and for instrumental assistance. Hopefully, this information will help you understand possible reasons for this greater attention, and will help you to have greater patience in offering CBPFA. CBPFA providers can play an active role in facilitating the recovery process and helping people of all ages adaptively cope after experiencing a traumatic stressor.

Acknowledgment

A special contribution by Lisa M. Brown, PhD, ABPP. Dr Brown is a Professor and Director of the Trauma Program at Palo Alto University. She is a nationally renowned authority on psychological support for older adults.

16

COMMUNITY-BASED PSYCHOLOGICAL FIRST AID WITH MARGINALIZED COMMUNITIES

B.A. Boyd
University of South Dakota, Vermillion, SD, United States

Community-based psychological first aid (CBPFA) is a naturally good fit for work in ethnic minority and other marginalized communities. Because of the grassroots nature of this approach, it lends itself well to adaptation in cultures that differ from the mainstream. This chapter will provide an overview of the issues involved in recognizing the culture of an affected community, how culture may affect the expression of distress following a crisis or disaster situation, and the provision of CBPFA in marginalized communities.

Community-Based Psychological First Aid. http://dx.doi.org/10.1016/B978-0-12-804292-2.00016-8

CBPFA helps participants use the skills they already have to provide basic psychological support to people who have been adversely affected by disaster, tragedy, crisis, or other traumatic event. Help is provided by friends, family members, neighbors, colleagues, and others who may also have been affected by the crisis situation. CBPFA happens where the people are: in shelters, in hospitals, evacuation center, waiting rooms, waiting lines, food service areas, and people's homes. CBPFA normalizes common reactions to traumatic (overwhelming) events and helps survivors find effective ways to cope with the ongoing stress of the crisis situation. Although witnessing a traumatic event will have some sort of impact on everyone, if people receive adequate psychological support in the aftermath of the event, most people will not need specialized mental health care. When that psychological support is provided by the survivor's natural support system, it may be as powerful for the survivor's recovery process as professional mental health services. In addition, by occurring within the natural support system, and in the survivor's natural frame of reference and understanding of the world, it has the best chance of being responsive to the cultural needs of the survivor.

What is Culture?

Culture can be defined in many ways and there is no one universally agreed upon definition. The Cambridge Dictionary Online defines culture as: "the way of life of a particular people, esp. as shown in their ordinary behavior and habits, their attitudes toward each other, and their moral and religious beliefs" (http://dictionary.cambridge.org/us/dictionary/english/culture). Culture tells us the reason for our being, the ways that we need to be in life, the expectations we have of ourselves and each other, and the ways that we relate to each other. Although when we think of culture, we tend to think of celebrations, food, dance, songs, and other visible forms of culture, culture, in fact, goes much deeper than this. Culture affects every aspect of our existence. It defines the relationship between genders, how we view children and the elderly, how we expect respect to be shown, what concepts such as time, success, wellness and healing mean to us, patterns of coping, methods of resolving conflict, the cadence of oral language, the appropriate amount of personal space, etc.

We begin to learn about our culture in our earliest days, in our smallest circles of contact, in those places we think of as "home." In these places, we learn how the world is, what we expect from others, how we are expected to behave, how we expect others around us to look, to behave, etc. As we grow older, our circles of contact grow wider and more diverse. But our basic expectations of how we understand the world remain very much the same.

Culture also frames how people experience disaster or tragedy, how we decide the meaning of the event, what is considered to be traumatic, how traumatic stress is manifested, what is seen as help, and how one will know they are whole again. "Help" will not be considered useful unless it is consistent with our own cultural understanding of what help should be, who should give it, what it should be focused on accomplishing, who should receive it first, etc. In times of crisis, culture defines support, helps to guide behavior, and provides the template for how recovery should look. Culture is evident in all interactions, whether we are aware of it or not. If we are unaware that we, ourselves, are cultural beings, or that we approach new experiences from within our own cultural framework, we may be unable to recognize that survivors are responding from within their own cultural frameworks as well. These issues become very important when we think about what it means to provide help and support to someone who has experienced a traumatic event.

Being a Helper

Becoming a helper can mean different things in different cultures. In the mainstream culture of the United States., it often means having a specific title and official role (often as a professional) that is understood by the people in the community. However, in an ethnocultural community (a community that shares both ethnic status and longstanding culture) or other marginalized community, there may be a strong cultural component to who is considered a "helper." It *may* include official or professional helpers (eg, community leaders, emergency responders, medical personnel, etc.), but it may also include community-specific "natural helpers" such as elders, hairdressers, bartenders, business owners, or others to whom people typically turn in times of need in that community. It might also include a spiritual/ceremonial leader, a community speaker or representative, or someone who speaks on behalf of the leadership. In situations, where natural helpers are working along with professional helpers to assist a community, it is important to remember that the natural helpers are every bit as important in getting the work done, and may be even more important in terms of understanding what help is needed and what it should look like.

Photographer: Euodia Chua.

Understanding Traumatic Stress

Traumatic stress can affect many aspects of a person's life. But it is also important to understand that many aspects of the way a person experiences traumatic events is affected by culture. Culture affects what is seen as traumatic, how one interprets the meaning of the traumatic event, prescribes the way that one must heal, and how it looks to become "whole" again.

As you have seen in previous chapters, traumatic stress has an impact on every aspect of one's being. It affects emotions (eg, denial, fear, anxiety, anger sadness, guilt), thoughts (eg, disorientation, confusion, limited attention span, memory problems, difficulty setting priorities), bodies (eg, increased blood pressure, respirations, and heartbeat, stomach distress, headaches, muscle aches, exaggerated startle response, fatigue, tunnel vision), and spirits (eg, feeling the world has turned upside down, loss of a sense of meaning, crisis of faith), and effects in any of these areas can have an effect on behaviors (eg, increased or decreased activity, sleep, and appetite, difficulty communicating, changes in performance, hypervigilance, increased use of substances).

Although the individual expressions of traumatic stress differ widely across cultures some reactions seem to be fairly consistent. These include:

- concern for the basic survival of self and loved ones;
- feelings of grief over the death of loved ones and loss of valued and meaningful possessions;

- the experience of fear and anxiety about safety of self and loved ones;
- sleep disturbances, including nightmares and imagery from the traumatic event;
- concern about relocation; and
- a need to feel one is part of the community and its recovery efforts.

It is important to understand that the way people *express* traumatic stress, fear, grief, and loss might be very different across cultures. In some cultures, it is common for grief to be endured quietly with no overt expression of sadness or loss. In other cultures, it might be expected that one would wail and throw themselves upon the body, the casket, or the grave. And, of course, there are many possible expressions along the continuum between these two points. Some cultures and belief systems demand that one who has died should be buried immediately and others require that a certain period of time passes before final disposition of the body. Rituals and ceremonies are conducted by prescribed members of the community, and certain other members of the community or family play prescribed roles of their own. A return to wholeness takes a prescribed amount of time, during which the grieving family members perform certain tasks to help themselves or their departed loved one during the time of mourning, and in order to emerge from the grieving process.

Community Reactions to Traumatic Stress

Disasters are not just individual events; they are also community events. Much like individuals, communities may also experience the effects of traumatic stress following a disaster or other terrible event in the community. There may be a communal experience of shock, disbelief, grief or anger (*emotional*), disorientation (*cognitive*), nonconstructive, or even destructive, behaviors (*behavioral*), and struggles to make sense of what has happened (*spiritual*) (Boyd, Quevillon, & Engdahl, 2010). In the best of situations, a community will come to see itself as a stronger, more cohesive, resilient version of itself. But, this depends, in large part, on the degree that help and interventions contribute to making the event manageable, whether those resources are sufficient to the need, and whether the community can successfully reframe the traumatic event into a challenge that can be successfully overcome (Zinner & Williams, 1999).

Disproportionate Impact

No one who has experienced a disaster is untouched by it, but the impact of disasters is often disproportionately harmful to ethnic minority and other marginalized communities (Marsalla, Johnson, Watson, & Gryczynski, 2008). People from diverse cultures, individuals with limited proficiency in the mainstream language (eg, English in the United States), individuals with disabilities, the homeless, the elderly, children, and those who are transportation-disadvantaged often have additional risk factors that may cause them to experience disproportionate effects of traumatic events, and which may make it more challenging to fully recover from a disaster (U.S. Department of Health & Human Services, 2008). People living in rural areas, particularly those marginalized by poverty or ethnocultural status, and survivors of political repression, genocide, or displacement, may also have a heightened risk in times of crisis (Institute of Medicine, 2003). Disasters, regardless of type, are detrimental to the existing protective mechanisms of social groups and tend to exacerbate preexisting community tensions and problems with social injustice and inequality (IASC, 2007).

The most economically or culturally marginalized communities are at greatest risk for disruptions in the healing process after a disaster occurs (Cox & Perry, 2011). These communities are often less prepared, have fewer resources available for help, are more likely to suffer devastating effects, and experience a much slower recovery process overall (Laborde, Brannock, & Parrish, 2011). When those who propose to be of help in the aftermath of a disaster lack adequate knowledge, awareness, or skills to respond to the specific cultural and language needs of marginalized communities, further damage may be done.

Cumulative Traumatic Stresses

For many marginalized communities, the current disaster is not the first event to stress the community resources. Some communities have had a long history of resource loss, dislocation, discrimination, isolation, and lack of access to outside support and resources. While previous experience of traumatic stress may make an individual or a community stronger and more able to survive a new event, marginalized individuals and communities are less likely to have received adequate help in the past and, consequently, are less likely to be thriving when a new disaster occurs. In many marginalized communities, there is a greater likelihood that the long-term effects of poverty, discrimination, unemployment, and oppression have had a traumatizing effect even before the "disaster" occurs. Similarly, when a disaster continues to have an impact long after the actual event has occurred (eg, people do not have permanent housing for months or years after the event), it is important to recognize the ways in which individuals and communities continue to suffer far beyond the actual occurrence of the identified disaster.

When a disaster occurs on top of the experience of multiple traumatic events, the effects of the disaster may be magnified and multiplied. Consequently, any help that the community receives only scratches the surface of the wounds that need to be healed. To make the situation worse, the Western cultural lens often leads outside helpers to "diagnose" and look for "disorders." When helpers come from outside the community and do not understand the many ways in which the community is experiencing and expressing traumatic stress, the community may be seen as "pathological" rather than "wounded," "grieving," or simply experiencing social injustices. When a community has had previous experiences with such inadequate outside "helpers," where help given has not resulted in anything truly helpful, the community may become suspicious of helpers, distrustful of outsiders, and unlikely to ask for help in times of crisis. In return, those on the outside may come to blame the community for its own social problems, and overlook the enormous social injustices and traumatic events that have taken place over time and across generations. The interaction of these processes is what has marginalized the community in the first place. In order to be of help in the aftermath of disasters and other traumatic events, those providing help will need to understand these communities in new ways. This is why it is so important for help to come from within the community itself. One important first step is for community members to become skilled in providing CBPFA.

Active Listening

You have learned about the skills involved in providing CBP-FA generally. This part of the chapter will discuss how that might be different in communities which are different from the mainstream.

Active listening is the central skill in CBPFA. As with everything else, the way to show that one is listening, and the way one interprets the verbal and nonverbal communication of others, varies a great deal across cultures. Some of those differences will be demonstrated in the descriptions subsequently. But it should be remembered that, although the actual details might change across different cultures, the general concepts are similar and can be used across all cultures. Because CBPFA is deeply rooted in each community where it is practiced, it ensures that interventions are responsive to the cultural needs of the community.

BESTT

Returning to the BESTT EARS acronym, we start by looking at the nonverbal aspects of communication. Body language, like any other language, is dependent on culture and there are many different ways of communicating our attentiveness, empathy, understanding, or caring. Something as simple as how you sit in relation to another person can be very different from one culture to another. In some cultures, it may feel perfectly comfortable to sit knee-to-knee looking directly at another person. In other cultures, this would be much too intense and might even feel intrusive. Things like eye contact and personal space are very much affected by culture and can vary widely, even for people within the same culture. The variations might seem to be overwhelming; however, the good news is that these are things we notice and adjust our behaviors to accommodate, without even consciously thinking about it most of the time. If we are standing too close to someone or gazing too intently at them, we can feel their discomfort, and we automatically adjust our distance or our gaze. If we can tell someone feels disconnected from us, we may need to move closer, lean in, or intensify our gaze to make them feel that we are truly engaged with them. We use nods of the head, small movements, or vocal sounds to let people know that we are still listening, encourage them to continue talking, convey our sympathy, or simply let them know we care. Sometimes the use of touch may be used to convey these points but, this, too, is subject to many rules of culture, cultural etiquette, gender and age roles, etc. In addition, if the person has experienced a traumatic event, and especially if it was violent, the use of touch must be used very cautiously regardless of culture.

EARS

Culture has an effect on the verbal aspects of communication as well. Encouragement is often about helping people find the strength to continue or to find positive meaning in tragic events. The things that we can say to encourage another will likely be different from one culture to another. For example, in an individualistic culture, one might say something like, "You are going to get through this. You can do it." On the other hand, in a more collective culture, words of encouragement might be more reflective of how the person is not alone, is part of something larger than themselves, or should look to their relatives to help get them through the difficult time. Similarly, belief systems help to define how people will view what has happened to them and what is appropriate to say to encourage them to move forward. Cultures and belief systems have an impact on the kinds of attributions one might make for difficult times. For some, challenges may be due to something one has done or not done, and the most encouraging words will be reminding the person about the will of a higher being. In other belief systems, where the goal is to overcome adversity, words of encouragement will be about finding strength to go forward.

As in all good CBPFA, part of verbal active listening is paraphrasing, summarizing, and asking questions to make sure that you understand. The nuances of this will always reflect culture and, again, we all make these adjustments all the time, often without consciously thinking about it. When listening to someone from another culture, the best course of action is to follow their lead in terms of style, timing, cadence, etc. If it feels as though you are not connecting with the person you are trying to help, sometimes the best thing you can do is to ask what is appropriate. Seek guidance from others who know the culture or simply ask the person how it might look if they were to help someone. When people are hurting or grieving or sad, what they need most is to feel connection to others who care. Knowing that someone is reaching out to them with kindness and caring can bridge even cultural gaps in times of tragedy.

Coping Skills

Although most people find ways to cope following a disaster, it is not surprising that survivors' functioning would be somewhat diminished as they process the events around them emotionally, cognitively, physiologically, and spiritually. Often, survivors simply need support and reassurance that their reactions are the normal effects of the traumatic events they have experienced, and that they will feel better with time. Being able to identify, label, and put into words the reactions they are experiencing is very helpful to survivors. Sharing with people that they are having normal reactions to an abnormal situation can be very comforting to survivors who feel they do not have control of anything—including their reactions.

Many times, people who have experienced a disaster believe that they are the only one who has been affected in that way. They may not recognize that even the people closest to them are experiencing similar reactions. It may be very helpful for them to hear that what they are experiencing is normal, and that others are likely experiencing those feelings as well. Helping them to remember how they, or their people, have coped with difficult situations in the past, can help them to engage familiar ways of coping. The sooner that survivors reconnect to their usual coping and systems of support and healing, the faster their healing process will begin, and the better they will be able to provide support to others in their communities.

Getting Additional Help

As you have read in previous chapters, there are times when active listening is not enough to help people cope in the aftermath of a traumatic event. There are times when people really do need additional help. It may be because they were already experiencing grief, loss, or mental illness. They may have extra risk factors for experiencing debilitating effects of traumatic stress. Whatever the reason, it is important to recognize when someone's needs are beyond what you can handle. In some cases, that help will be professional mental health care. In other cases, the additional help may be culturally-determined.

The concept of "help," itself, is culturally determined and culture affects both the giver and the recipient. What may seem "helpful" in the giver's culture may not be seen as anything of the sort in the recipient's culture. It is important for the help-giver to keep in mind that the sole reason for being in that "helping" role is to provide assistance to those affected by the crisis situation. It becomes imperative to understand what is meant by help in the recipient's cultural view, who that help should come from, who else should be there, who can sanction it, what it would look like, what the expected response would be, how to know when to stop, etc. Because no one is able to know these nuances of every culture, it also becomes important to find the resources within the affected community that can inform and sanction outside help. The culture will also define how "recovery" will eventually look. Again, it is those from inside the community who will be most knowledgeable about the form that help should take.

Making it Relevant for the Community

Healing is a communal process. Because traumatic events can make survivors think they are alone, one of the most important elements of healing for survivors of traumatic events is helping them to reconnect to their natural support systems and to invoke their natural healing mechanisms. In marginalized communities, this can mean helping people reconnect to their traditional cultures as sources of healing and wellness. The traditional culture and practices of a community have sustained and supported the people for generations. It can be an important source of strength, comfort, and healing in times of crisis. Helping people who are hurting to focus on the supports of their culture, community, and belief system can be the most important things a helper can do.

Conclusions

Cultures do not remain the same. They are dynamic. They change and adapt, allowing them to endure over time and through situations we cannot anticipate. Crisis often provides new opportunities for growth, healing, and change. Many communities have grown and become stronger through their experience of hardship and adversity. As helpers, if we are aware of those potential opportunities, we can help survivors and survivor communities to grow, adapt, and move into the future as stronger, more resilient, versions of themselves. CBPFA gives us a template for providing support to others while encouraging them to stay connected to the stabilizing foundation of their culture.

Acknowledgment

A special contribution by Beth A. Boyd, PhD. Dr Boyd is Professor of Psychology and Director of the APA-accredited doctoral Clinical Psychology Training Program at the University of South Dakota. She is also a nationally renowned authority on ethnic minority psychology and an enrolled member of the Seneca tribe.

References

Boyd, B., Quevillon, R. P., & Engdahl, R. (2010). Working with rural and diverse communities after disasters. In P. Dass-Brailsford (Ed.), *Crisis and disaster counseling: Lessons learned from Hurricane Katrina and other disasters. Thousand.* Oaks, CA: Sage.

Cox, R. S., & Perry, K. E. (2011). Like a fish out of water: reconsidering disaster recovery and the role of place and social capital in community disaster resilience. *American Journal of Community Psychology, 48*(3–4), 395–411.

Institute of Medicine (2003). *Preparing for the psychological consequences of terrorism: A public health strategy.* Washington, DC: The National Academies Press.

Inter-Agency Standing Committee (IASC) (2007). *IASC guidelines on mental health and psychosocial support in emergency settings.* Geneva: IASC.

Laborde, D. J., Brannock, K., & Parrish, T. (2011). Assessment of training needs for disaster mental health preparedness in black communities. *Journal of the National Medical Association, 103*(7), 624–634.

Marsella, A., Johnson, J. L., Watson, P., & Gryczynski, J. (2008). In A. J. Marsella, J. L. Johnson, P. Watson, & J. Gryczynski (Eds.), *Ethnocultural perspectives on disaster and trauma: Foundations, issues, and applications* (pp. 3–13). New York: Springer.

U.S. Department of Health and Human Services. Disaster mental health recommendations: report of the Disaster Mental Health Subcommittee of the National Biodefense Science Board. (2008). http://www.phe.gov/Preparedness/legal/boards/nprsb/Documents/nsbs-dmhreport-final.pdf.

Zinner, E. S., & Williams, M. B. (1999). Summary and incorporation: a reference frame for community recovery and restoration. In E. S. Zinner, & M. B. Williams (Eds.), *When a Community Weeps: Case Studies in Survivorship.* Philadelphia, PA: Brunner/Mazel.

17

COMMUNITY-BASED PSYCHOLOGICAL FIRST AID WITH RURAL COMMUNITIES

R.P. Quevillon

University of South Dakota, Vermillion, SD, United States

The CBPFA described in this book is a method of providing support that takes into account the community and social context of the person in need. As seen throughout this volume, individual and community-based adaptations of CBPFA are expected and desirable. Whenever a person offers psychological support to another, sensitivity to the person's worldview, cultural background, and unique characteristics is important. This chapter is based on the assumptions that rural communities form a context worthy of a CBPFA adaptation and that, indeed, rural areas are extremely well-suited to the CBPFA approach. Therefore, the present chapter seeks to provide background in some of the elements of rural life. In doing so, it can hopefully be useful to those seeking to provide CBPFA support to rural dwellers and also be helpful to someone wishing to develop a rural community-based program, leading to a local CBPFA network in a rural community.

The concept of rural has been unusually hard to define with consistency, reflecting a number of different governmental conceptions and sets of rules. Certainly, sparse population is the key concept and distance from metropolitan areas is also a factor. The term "frontier area," often defined as having less than two

Community-Based Psychological First Aid. http://dx.doi.org/10.1016/B978-0-12-804292-2.00017-X

people per square mile, is also used, but here we will simply employ the term rural. An important initial thing to remember when considering rural areas is that there is a tremendous variety of the rural experience and that one community will very much differ from another reflecting economic, cultural, geographic, religious, and a host of other factors. Much of my experience has been within rural America, so my expertise is strongest there. However, diversity is still the rule rather than the exception for rural areas, even within the United States. Despite all the diversity, there are generalizations that can be made with at least a fair amount of confidence. Knowing these general points should prove useful when working with rural dwellers and in planning for rural CBPFA programs, particularly if one is open to exceptions and is aware of the need to always assess the quality of one's assumptions.

Characteristics of Rural Communities

One of the factors to consider in aiding your understanding of rural communities is economics. Rural communities will certainly differ in their economic bases. One community may emphasize farming, another may primarily rely on mining, and a third location may center on ranching. But most rural communities share the characteristic of a less diversified economic base as compared with more populated areas. This tends to make them more susceptible to economic changes or challenges, having much less cushion against economic downturn, like rocking in a small boat leaves one much more susceptible to being buffeted by the waves. Poverty is also a problem. Nationally, rural areas have more families and individuals living in poverty than typical metropolitan areas. The problem that poverty poses for adjustment and coping is enormous. A simple stressor like noticing your tire is flat as you leave for work can be just a minor blip if all you have to do is take your other car. However it can be turned into an imposing test of personal resourcefulness if you are without the ready instrumental supports. You might be juggling child care, risking job loss, and/or bartering for repairs in a much more stressful situation.

In addition, rural family economics tend to be made more challenging by the fact of increased distances and reduced services that are characteristic of rural areas. Most services, particularly specialized ones, are much less easily available to rural dwellers. The waiting times and often the expenses, travel problems, scheduling hassles, and the like tend to be greater than that in urban areas. Things like plumbing or heating problems might take on increased pressure and the greater distance in traveling to specialists, such as medical providers, adds expense and scheduling hassles. Having to wait longer for emergency medical assistance or for a hazardous-materials team to arrive might have disastrous consequences.

Another shared aspect of many rural communities is the small town social structure. Rural dwellers tend to experience less change in their social networks than their urban counterparts. They have social networks that tend to be smaller (fewer people) but with more multiple connections to network members (higher density). There are fewer available people in sparsely populated areas to serve in the various roles, so one is more likely to have a co-worker as a friend and serve with them (or a family member of theirs) on the school board, or in the Optimist club, or have them as a coach on your daughter's softball team.

It is worth repeating that not all rural communities have these dense social networks and relatively less turnover as compared to metropolitan areas, but when this social structure is present, it has numerous implications for rural individuals. First, the simple fact of fewer strangers being present makes them stand out more, and become more noticeable. Rural people tend to be used to going places where most of the faces are recognizable. For many, this is a pleasant, even comforting, situation, but it directs more attention to strangers and may even contribute to the fact that folks in rural areas tend to have a heightened mistrust of outsiders. Indeed, gaining acceptance into a rural community can be painfully slow. I am reminded of some work I did in a small town in the Midwest which had me attending several meetings with the local business leaders. One fellow, who owned a shoe store, was never addressed by name and was known only as "the new guy." I later found out that he had been running his business in that village for more than 10 years! In some places, full acceptance may take an extremely long time, even requiring multiple generations in some cases.

Another implication of the social structure in sparsely populated areas is something called "business by personal relationships." That is, because rural dwellers often have considerable personal information and direct experience with those with whom they deal, they are inclined to put a lot of stock in the person's reputation, history, and especially how that person has come across to them. Some of the traditional factors, such as formal role, official position, and academic/professional credentials tend to carry less weight than they do in the bigger cities. I routinely introduce myself with my nickname and last name, rather than my formal "Dr Quevillon" moniker when meeting folks from rural areas.

A final community characteristic to be covered here is that of the "fishbowl" effect. In some rural areas, residents have a strong sense that others in their environment are aware of them and are paying attention to what they do. Naturally, this can be a positive experience for some, a troublesome feeling for others, or both, depending on the situation. Rural children can sometimes feel that it is nearly impossible to get away from the watchful eyes of adults and that their parents will hear about any misstep. This sense that others in your community are attending to you, are concerned about you, and are paying attention to what you do can be very positive. For many rural dwellers, it contributes to a sense of community, a feeling of belonging, shared values, and emotional connection that, while not unique to rural areas by any means, tends to flourish in rural communities. For many parts of the rural United States, sense of community is a clear factor in residents' perceived well-being and reported satisfaction with their lives. But the "fishbowl" can have negative effects on some community members. Some rural people experience the attention and scrutiny of others as judgmental and harsh. They might experience negative opinions based on actions of relatives or even their ancestors. They consequently do not feel a sense of community with those around them and sometimes may feel that the gossip and negative perceptions of them will persist no matter what they do. Feeling judged and alienated, their stress is often made worse by the knowledge that others nearby are part of a cohesive unit.

Rural Values

Many experts, such as sociologist Morton Wagenfeld, have maintained for several years that rural/urban values differences are shrinking, in part due to the broad access that most persons have to national media (Wagenfeld, 2003). However, my experience has been that generalizations about rural values are still fairly useful, especially if one remains open to the many exceptions that you will come across. As always, it is crucial to keep an open mind and to continuously assess your assumptions, to see if they are well-founded.

One common value in much of rural America is that of self-reliance. Rural individuals take pride in their independence and value their ability to get things done by themselves, without outside assistance. While the value of self-reliance works well for mobilizing a person's efforts to cope actively and effectively with stressful situations, it may also get in the way of someone seeking help or support if they really need it. Further, valuing self-reliance in one's neighbors can be a source of community pride, but it can also lead to negative judgments about others' help-seeking, perhaps contributing to the stigma, or sense of disgrace, that can accompany the act of seeking support.

Related to self-reliance is the concept of individualism, which is often linked to rural dwellers. Individualism is often described as the value stance that emphasizes individual goals and achievements as compared to collectivism where group identity, goals, and achievements are paramount. However, our research and experience with rural groups has taught us that it is not so simple. In the past, social scientists have tended to put individualism and collectivism on opposite ends of a continuum, suggesting that if you have a high degree of individualism, you would be low in collectivism, or vice versa. Our work has suggested that the concepts are much more independent—that a given individual could be high on both, low on both, and so on. Many rural dwellers, especially the farm families with whom we have worked, are often high in both individualism and collectivism. They value individual achievements and self-reliance, but also have a strong sense of community and feel invested in and connected to the people around them. As seen throughout this book, when teaching people about CBPFA it is important to talk about the helper role and to impress upon them that they can assume the role of helper and that doing so would provide important social support to those around them. When teaching CBPFA to rural groups, I try to tap into collectivist values by bring up the notion of being a good neighbor and how PFA can help provide some of the tools to make for better neighbors.

A related, but distinct, value is the value placed on family. While not exclusive to rural areas by any means, a strong valuing of family ties and connections across generations is clearly present in a great many rural individuals. A sense of family history and familial traditions, as well as a strong feeling of responsibility to past and future generations often form guiding concepts for rural dwellers. Other common cornerstones include spiritual life and the person's religious community. Rural individuals tend to hold more conservative religious views than their urban counterparts as well as more conservative political and social views. These values may well help some individuals feel grounded and connected to their communities and traditions, thus solidifying their sense of community.

However, the same values that can be reassuring in their consistency can also make rural individuals susceptible to some values-rooted distress. As mentioned previously, rural individuals tend to have a more pronounced mistrust of outsiders than many urban groups. Further, it is pretty common for rural dwellers to hold, to some degree, a fatalistic view of their world and future. That is, they view many of the major factors determining what happens to them and will happen in the future as being things outside of their control. They have less of the notion of being the authors of their own futures through their actions and attitudes and more of a sense of being buffeted by outside influences, over which they have no control. It is not clear why this is the case. Possibly, it may be rooted in part in the fact that rural dwellers are often more immersed in outside influences, such as seeing weather events ruin crops or change travel plans, or having governmental policies (perceived as coming from afar) make major changes in their lives. Whatever might be the complex of contributing factors, this fatalism can, for some, be a source of considerable distress, especially if combined with other negative perceptions. Along that line, it seems to be a bit easier for individuals in rural areas to feel alienated, apart from the mainstream, and somewhat out of step with current societal developments. All of these factors, and more, have seemingly come together to produce for some, a distressing sense that their lives are changing for the worse and that their valued ways are slipping away. This feeling of alienation and uncomfortable change is not solely felt by rural individuals of course, but it is likely made more prominent by characteristics of rural life and of rural dwellers.

The Case for Rural CBPFA

In this chapter, I take the dual positions that, not only is CBPFA a viable method of providing psychological and social support to rural individuals, but CBPFA is in some ways truly an excellent fit with many aspects of rural communities and their citizens. I am convinced that there exists no single method or approach that can singlehandedly take care of the stress-reduction needs of any community. Therefore having many alternative sources of assistance is always necessary. CBPFA can provide one of these alternatives, and in doing so, raise the capacity of a rural community to provide support for its members.

Photographer: Gerard Jacobs.

There is no doubt that folks in rural areas, just like people everywhere, have plenty of stress with which to cope. When I was growing up, I heard some people espouse what I call the "Golden Rural Myth"—the mistaken notion that rural settings are places of "clean air, hard work, and virtually no stress." Unfortunately, the facts refute the no-stress part absolutely. For example, in the many studies of diagnosable mental health and substance use problems, the rates in rural and urban areas are very comparable across a wide array of conditions. Virtually the only exceptions are that rural areas are likelier to have pockets of exceptionally high rates of abuse of specific substances, like methamphetamines, and that suicide rates are generally higher in rural areas. The suicide rates, which are generally alarming, but especially so for older rural male residents and Native American youth, provide a grim rebuttal to the "Golden Rural Myth."

Of course, stress and stress reactions affect many more persons than those experiencing diagnosable conditions like those aforementioned. Individuals living in rural areas can face numerous stressors and challenges, some of which stem from community characteristics and impacts that rural life can have on values, stances, and attitudes (Smalley, Warren, & Rainer, 2012). As touched on before, a sense of alienation can form, a heightened sense of distance from outsiders and even a feeling of being embattled and losing one's lifestyle or traditions. In addition, the sparse population, geographical distance, transportation issues, and some of the physical settings can engender feelings of loneliness and isolation. Rural dwellers are often more attuned to the environment than many urbanites. They often have a more acute sense of place than others, being more aware of both the built environment and, most especially, the natural setting. This sense of place is typically a positive aspect of people's lives. People can often enjoy the beauty of a setting or find comfort in the familiarity of environmental features. But a heightened sense of place can also make a person more susceptible to negative associations, such as fears, that may come from dramatic negative events at the site. Furthermore, catastrophes such as fires, floods, tornadoes, or hurricanes can dramatically alter the features of a place, and individuals with a heightened sense of place often feel the loss of the familiar place more acutely than those less attuned. In addition, people living in rural environments may also experience stress from the disruption of familiar places from planned events such as mining, forestry, or the like. Imagine the possible distress if your community, for economic reasons, decided to permit a landfill or toxic waste site in place of landforms that had been part of your life for as long as you can remember!

As we have discussed, a sense of community is typically a strong contributor for the well-being of people everywhere, but it is often particularly strongly felt in rural communities. The down side, of course, is feeling left out or judged by those around you, a stressful situation experienced by some. The "fishbowl" effect, that sense of the people around you attending to you and taking note of what you do, can worsen the feeling of being harshly judged or excluded. Clearly this can be a major stressor for some people in rural communities. The stigma associated with help-seeking is a related issue. It is difficult for people in rural areas to seek help, particularly for issues of stress or psychological distress, because of several factors. These include the common value on self-reliance, concern about judgmental attitudes of others, and common attitudes that downplay psychological influences and emphasize external forces shaping one's life (fatalism). With pressure coming from community members, and often from the individual themselves, to avoid outsider assistance, having alternatives within the community, such as CBPFA, takes on even more importance. Seeking formal help from outside is difficult because of availability and access issues as well as the stigma and acceptability problems just presented. Therefore, CBPFA with its basis in community members providing the support, is an outstanding alternative for rural individuals. It gives the community an acceptable and accessible way to support its citizens.

The final individual factor in the case for CBPFA relates to social networks. It was mentioned previously that individuals in sparsely populated settings often have social networks that are dense—comprised of fewer individuals but with many more connections to each network member. Implications of dense networks tend to be that they intensify the fishbowl feeling (people knowing a lot about you through the multiple connections), but this type of network can also be helpful in that the multiple connections make it likelier that someone will notice a person in need. Because some individuals withdraw when highly stressed, dense social networks can help avoid someone falling between the cracks and failing to be supported. A final offshoot of the dense social network common to rural areas is that, because of the relatively small size and high density, widespread and/or catastrophic events are more likely to overwhelm the network than is the case in larger, less inter-connected systems. In effect, this makes many rural area challenged when it comes to disasters. Because disasters are often widespread, with ripple effects on those indirectly affected, rural networks are often hit hard and do not have enough individuals to support their fellows. I have often heard Jerry Jacobs, this book's author, talk about the time he was called to provide disaster mental health assistance to a small community that was hit with a catastrophic fire, producing several casualties, many injuries and considerable property damage. Issues for this community included the fact that many responders and service/support personnel were related to or closely connected to victims; responders and support personnel were related to or intimately connected to other responders; virtually all community members were related or closely connected to responders, victims, and support personnel—in short everyone was impacted. While the community was temporarily unable to muster the coping resources to deal with the tragedy; they were a community well versed in mutual assistance and were very able to make use of the outside support to build their capacity to assist themselves. Communities, such as this one, are common in rural areas and they have the potential to make excellent use of CBPFA training to increase the support capacity of the area.

In addition to the individual challenges faced by persons living in rural areas, some community characteristics can also challenge the support of rural citizens and the dissipation of stress. As we have noted, economics is a particular problem in rural communities. In addition to the high rates of poverty in many rural communities, the low tax base that results from poor and sparse populations has led to a widespread lack of resources in most rural areas that includes mental health and social service coverage. The accessibility of services, due to distances, transportation issues, such as weather and inferior roads, and the added expenses and scheduling difficulties makes seeking outside sources of help difficult. Also, specialized help is often less available to rural dwellers. The maps depicting the professional shortage areas for South Dakota, my home state, regarding medical providers and also mental health providers are literally maps of the whole state with the exception of small islands corresponding to Sioux Falls and Rapid City. In addition, we live in an era when national and state services are in a decline. The clear trend is to increase the reliance on local resources in response to disasters and related events.

So, clearly, there is substantial need for support and stress relief for rural individuals and circumstances such as difficulties in getting outside support (and rural residents' resistance in seeking such support) make the building of local capacity to support community members all the more appealing. CBPFA, by its grassroots nature, is an ideal way to build that capacity and it is, because of its "good neighbor" structure, the style of helping that will be readily accepted by rural dwellers.

Photographer: Gerard Jacobs.

TRY THIS

If you are wishing to gain an initial sense of what a rural community is like, you might seek out the local café or eatery at lunchtime. Many rural villages have a place, usually somewhere serving food, which is known to residents as a gathering spot and community hub. It is a place where folks can meet and socialize, and find out what is going on in their area. You can easily identify the community hub by the fact that it will be fairly crowded at noon, with several cars parked outside. I recommend that you go inside and start to talk to the people there. Be friendly and informal, but don't intrude. Show your interest in the people and the area. It helps if you have done your homework, looking up some information about the community, its history, economic base, and so on. Be prepared also to answer questions about who you are and why you want to know about the area. I would simply state that you are interested in how people come together to support each other and wonder how the process works in this community. Above all, be respectful and patient. Residents will share what they wish to share at their desired pace. You will enjoy a hearty lunch and likely get an initial "feel" for the community. Hint: complement the food, do not be picky or difficult, and leave a normal tip.

Recommendations

To be sure, the suggestions throughout this book and in the appendix are excellent points which in no way conflict with my recommendations for CBPFA in rural areas. The active listening skills described in several chapters are extremely important, and they bring me to my first point of emphasis: allow plenty of time for the person to feel comfortable with you. Rural individuals may find it difficult to begin to tell their story or to trust you. Patience on the part of the listener will pay large dividends. Furthermore, there is considerable value in simply sitting with the person in need of support—being there for them. The emotional support conveyed by the fact that you care enough and have the patience to simply sit with them sends a powerful message.

The second thing I recommend is to be genuine. Be yourself, down to earth, and practical. Most people from rural backgrounds are used to dealing with people on a matter-of-fact and personal basis. If you try to be too formal, or to fit some stylized conception of the helper role, it will likely come across as awkward and phony. Some self-disclosure can be helpful in reinforcing the "we're all in this together" perspective, but be careful not to overdo it. Remember that the focus is always on the person you are supporting.

Finally, be sensitive to the stigma that the person (or those in the individual's social network) may hold regarding stress symptoms and how it might make them feel ashamed to admit to common stress reactions, even something as common as sleep difficulties. Gently normalizing their experiences and being patient and accepting while they tell their story can convey powerful and timely support.

For working with groups, doing training and planning CBPFA programs in rural communities, a few additional recommendations are in order. The suggestions contained in Appendix A are particularly relevant here. It is critically important to "partner up," to reach out to the segments of the community to learn of the formal and informal community structures and potential stakeholders interested in the program's success. Even if you are extremely familiar with the community, one person cannot do it all in terms of understanding the subgroups and representing their interests and goals.

Also, you need to show your investment in the process and respect for the community. You may not be able to achieve membership but you can leave behind the mistrusted outsider role by expending the effort to find out about community culture, history, economics and the like. It might involve learning of the trappings of agribusiness. As an example, I had no concept of the process of "walking beans" (laboriously hand-weeding soybeans) until my first year in South Dakota.

Finally, being personal, informal, genuine, and straightforward is key. Rural individuals will likely get to know you quickly as they observe you in the "fishbowl." There is no place to hide, but it turns out that the typical rural community is a very comfortable place to be after all.

Summary

This chapter attempted to provide an overview of rural issues as they pertain to CBPFA, both providing individuals with needed support and considerations for program planning. It is my sincere belief that the CBPFA model provides a very good fit with community and individual characteristics common in rural areas and holds much promise as a useful method of alleviating stress and supporting rural individuals and families.

Acknowledgment

A special contribution by Randal P. Quevillon, PhD. Dr Quevillon is Professor of Psychology and Chair of the Department of Psychology at the University of South Dakota. He is a renowned specialist in the stress of rural communities.

References

Smalley, K. B., Warren, J. C., & Rainer, J. P. (2012). *Rural mental health: Issues, policies, and best practices*. New York: Springer.

Wagenfeld, M. O. (2003). A snapshot of rural America. In B. H. Stamm (Ed.), *Rural behavioral healthcare: An interdisciplinary guide*. Washington, DC: American Psychological Association.

18

CLOSING THOUGHTS

In closing, let me particularly highlight some keys to providing effective CBPFA. It does not make you a mental health professional. It is important to know when to turn to a mental health professional. It may be time to seek some professional assistance when:

1. Unpleasant symptoms last more than 4–6 weeks, despite good CBPFA, or
2. It becomes difficult to function effectively on the job, or at home, or at school, even after receiving good CBPFA, or
3. An individual feels concerned about his/her behaviors or emotions.

And the extensions which apply for you as providers:

4. If you suspect that a person poses a danger to themselves or others, you need to get additional help for the person. If the danger seems immediate, contact law-enforcement authorities as soon as possible. If it does not seem immediately threatening, you may choose to consult a mental health professional about the situation, or simply bring the person to be seen in a mental health facility.
5. If you feel that a client's difficulties are uncomfortably beyond your skill level, it is important to make a referral to a mental health professional.

Second, be aware of stress, including cumulative stress and traumatic stress, in both yourself and those around you. Remember that there can be a very wide variety of individual ordinary reactions to extraordinary events. It is important that people understand that their traumatic stress reactions are not a sign of weakness, but only of being human.

Third, try to use active listening to improve your communications with other people, both in your personal and professional life. Good communication can be a powerful tool in improving your relationships. Do not wait to use it until you want to provide CBPFA. Practicing it daily will improve your skills.

Fourth, follow good ethical practices, not just in CBPFA, but in your day-to-day life. Remember that much of your credibility as a CBPFA provider may be established by the respect people have for you in your daily interactions when nothing terrible is taking place. Respect the humanity of each person you meet; treat them

Community-Based Psychological First Aid. http://dx.doi.org/10.1016/B978-0-12-804292-2.00018-1

with respect and honor. That means respecting the privacy of communications not only in CBPFA but also in your daily life. If you have a reputation as a gossip in the community, you are unlikely to be trusted as a CBPFA provider. Having respect for those you support also means not taking advantage of those around you. Again, treating people with respect will have many benefits in your life, aside from helping you be effective in providing psychological support.

Finally, be sure to take care of yourself. If you manage your own stress effectively, it will not only improve your own life but will also enhance your ability to provide effective psychological support.

I hope you will experience CBPFA as an effective tool for managing your own hassles and major stressors in life, and for supporting your family, friends, neighbors, and coworkers as you work through difficult times in your lives. If you all can support one another through the difficult times, it will also strengthen your sense of community and togetherness when you celebrate the good times. On a day-to-day basis, active-listening skills can improve your communication in your personal relationships as well as in your professional relationships. This combination of effective psychological support and improved communication can then lead to a stronger, healthier, happier community and a better life for us all.

APPENDIX A

COMMUNITY-BASED ADAPTATION OF CBPFA

The techniques of PFA can be used to help oneself manage the stressors of life, or to support one's family or friends, or on another similarly personal scale. In such cases, each individual can modify their own application of CBPFA to fit with their own beliefs and worldview. It is merely important to understand CBPFA as best you can, and to understand the limitations of CBPFA, that is, when and how to make a referral to a mental health professional if the need arises.

But you may also wish to consider developing a community model of CBPFA for one or more communities. This chapter is intended to give some suggestions for trying to organize such a program and adapt the training for the specific communities to be served. I do not want you to think, however, that CBPFA can only exist within a program.

Community Programs

When I was working in India, I learned that the word "community" is used somewhat differently there than I was used to in the United States. Instead of referring to a geographic area, the word community was used to refer to a group of people who share common interests such as religion, ethnicity, culture, occupation, hobbies, or schools attended by the children. This is a profitable way to think about community when we talk about a community adaptation of CBPFA.

Community-based program design helps to make CBPFA most effective in providing psychological support in a culturally responsive way for a specific community or group of communities. Community-based means that the program is adapted to serve the needs of each group of people who share common interests. As part of that concept, the program needs to build on the strengths of the people and the culture. This is best achieved by using local representatives to design and maintain the program. Although mental health professionals from outside the community may be

Community-Based Psychological First Aid. http://dx.doi.org/10.1016/B978-0-12-804292-2.00019-3

able to provide significant expertise to assist in design and training, local members of the community can best guide the adaptations to make the program ideal for their specific community.

Sustainability

If one is going to invest the effort to develop a program, it makes sense that the program be sustainable. CBPFA is a fairly simple program to establish. It does not have to make many demands on its organizers or participants. CBPFA does not require very many financial resources. It can provide immediate improvement to relationships through improved communications and mutual support, and can enhance those relationships over time. These are factors that help CBPFA to be fairly easily sustainable. CBPFA has the basic building blocks necessary for a good community-based psychological support program. If you are interested in developing a program that can promote CBPFA training for your community, the next step is to adapt CBPFA for that program.

Before I describe my suggestions on a way to proceed, let me emphasize that there may be many suitable ways to develop a CBPFA network in your area. The following is not a blueprint of how you must proceed, but one possible means to an end.

Typically, when a group has started a CBPFA program, they have conducted an initial "Training of Trainers" (ToT) to develop a group of trainers to offer CBPFA classes to their community. Since an individual community may not be large enough for their own ToT, it may be profitable to gather a few communities to work together.

Community Committee

The first step in the development of a community-based model is to develop a community committee. The committee participants would be members of the targeted community. Their focus would be how the CBPFA model could be adapted to make best use of the strengths in the community's culture or worldview. Typically the members of the committee would study the CBPFA model and consult with a trainer well-experienced in CBPFA. In some cases, members of the committee may want to attend a CBPFA training to inform their decisions as they try to adapt the program to the community.

There is no magic in the exact composition of this committee. I would suggest, however, a few possible roles to think about filling on the committee. One role would be that of a mental health professional who can assist in ensuring that the CBPFA techniques being taught remain scientifically valid even through the process of adapting CBPFA to the targeted community. A second role would be someone who can understand the possible needs and strategies for cultural adaptation of the CBPFA. This person would usually be a community psychologist, a social psychologist, a sociologist, an anthropologist, or someone with a similar skill set.

A third role would be someone, or several people who can provide insight to the spiritual side of the community. A chaplain, minister, mullah, or other spiritual leader representing one or more of the spiritual groups in the community or communities may be ideal. It is not necessary to have every religion represented in the community committee. It is important, however, to have someone who knows at least the basics about each of the different spiritual groups in the targeted community.

In many cases, the focal community may not include people with these specific skill sets. In these cases, individuals with such knowledge and skill sets may be consulted by the community committee.

A fourth role is someone who understands the social networks of the area to be served. Many people think that this committee member needs to be a politician. But in most cases, you can probably find a community resident who seems to know everyone, and knows what is happening everywhere, but has no official capacity. These folks can be very helpful members of the committee. I remember working in one small town after a major fire. We needed someone who knew all the segments of the community, was trusted by residents, and could effectively communicate with everyone in town. Everyone I asked about possible residents to serve this role gave me the same name, the wife of one of the local ministers. Not the minister, mind you, but his wife. She was a wondrous resource in the recovery of the community.

Other members of the committee might be representatives of local nongovernmental organizations such as the local chapter of the American Red Cross, a local soup kitchen, homeless shelter, or other such organizations that serve the communities being targeted. It is useful to keep the committee fairly small, perhaps limiting it to 10 people or less, if you want to be able to actually make progress in developing the plan. Too many people can make for endless discussion, and can also lead to "groupthink," a social process in which groups can make very bad collective decisions.

Determining Local Referral Resources

As discussed earlier in the book, one of the extremely important issues with CBPFA is for participants to understand the limitations of CBPFA. It is critical to recognize when people are experiencing reactions or problems that are outside the realm of ordinary reactions to extraordinary events. These individuals may require referral to the traditional mental health system. A useful next step for the community committee is to develop a list of community mental health centers, faith-based clinics, and private providers in the area to which people may refer if they work with someone whose needs are beyond CBPFA. Knowing which of these resources use a sliding-scale fee system, or accept some pro-bono (ie, for the good of the community; clients served without charge) clients can also be useful. Many mental health professionals serve a small number of clients as a pro-bono contribution to the communities they serve, and therefore the cost of professional services may not be a hindrance to getting the help needed. Psychology encourages practitioners to perform pro-bono services for the communities where their practices are located.

Community Adaptation

One of the roles of the community committee is to guide the adaptation of CBPFA for the specific community. It might be useful to take a few moments to consider the kinds of adaptations that might be appropriate.

Serving Individuals?

I recently heard a leading humanitarian worker challenge the use of psychological support programs that provide support for individuals rather than entire family units simultaneously, or entire communities. The rationale of this speaker was that some cultures focus more on the health and welfare of families and communities than of individuals, so support for individuals should not be attempted.

It is certainly true that mainstream American culture is more focused on individuals than some other cultures. I have worked with family and community-centered cultures in various places. One of the things I have learned is that even intensely focused family or community-centered cultures, families and communities are made up of individuals. The reason that CBPFA is so effective in such cultures is that CBPFA is intended to build on and enhance the ability of the entire family or community to provide support for one another.

As was discussed in Chapter 4, people who are experiencing traumatic stress reactions may be able to do little to contribute to their own recovery and healing. But it is also true that individuals with traumatic stress reactions are unlikely to be able to contribute to the healing and recovery of their families or their communities. People who are not part of the solution *are* part of the problem. The recovery of the family and the community, therefore, benefits from or may even demand the recovery of the individuals that compose the family or the community. In CBPFA communities, there are many people to support those experiencing traumatic stress reactions. Moreover, understanding traumatic stress will help the members of the family and/or the community to avoid developing traumatic stress reactions.

Some Examples of Cultural Adaptation

A few years ago, I was asked to organize a group of speakers for a world psychology conference in Beijing, China. They asked me to choose speakers who could illustrate the variety of ways that CBPFA is adapted in different cultures. I invited four speakers from different parts of the world. All four had begun with the same basic concept of CBPFA, were run by local residents, and I had previously had the opportunity to consult with each of them.

One speaker was from Iceland, a small island nation fairly isolated in the far North Atlantic. They had developed the model to have both community-based CBPFA provided for the general population and disaster mental health services provided by mental health professionals when needed.

In Kenya, a psychological support program was developed to serve Kenyans affected by the 1998 bombing of the US embassy in Nairobi. When those who were directly affected in the bombing had been served, the program was adapted to serve Kenyans with HIV/AIDS.

In Turkey, a psychological support program was developed to serve those affected by the extensive devastating earthquake in 1999. The program was adapted to provide long-term CBPFA. In their model, the program rebuilt community centers in affected villages. Some of the staff hired to manage those community centers were mental health professionals. The community centers do all the traditional things that Turkish community centers did. They offered various courses to residents (eg, baking, sewing, gardening etc.) and added CBPFA to that list of courses. The mental health professionals were accepted in the communities as staff of the community center, and a welcome addition to the villages. The rental of the community hall for receptions and parties served to fund the ongoing program.

In Japan, they had developed their CBPFA model as a cross between CBPFA and a disaster mental health model, training medical-disaster response teams in psychological support. Some of these team members were mental health professionals, but most were medical professionals. Their strategy was that talking about psychological difficulties is not very acceptable in much of Japanese culture, and that the medical setting might be the most acceptable place to discuss psychological issues. So they initially based their psychological support program in the medical-response teams, with hopes that as the country began to accept psychological support in that context, they could begin to introduce CBPFA.

All four countries started with similar concepts, but adapted it to best fit their own culture at that point in time. In each case the development of the adaptation was done over a period of months with consultation from specialists in both psychological support and culture, and with representatives of local communities involved.

Similarly in Sri Lanka after the 2004 tsunami, PFA trainers met with community committees to adapt the program to the needs of local groups. Such a high percentage of the population of these areas had died in the tsunami that the people who had performed many roles in the community were no longer there. And in many cases, there was no one else who knew how to fulfill that role. Many of the community committees asked if the CBPFA preparation could include training one of the residents in how to perform the Buddhist "singing ceremony," which is an important ritual in their culture for coping with difficult times. The organizers contacted a Buddhist monastery, and the monks agreed to train some residents in each community how to perform the ceremony.

In Gujarat, India when I was helping them develop a CBPFA program following a major earthquake in 2001, we were planning community meetings. My local colleague asked who would be in charge of the dancing. I was confused, because I had never seen dance take place at a meeting on CBPFA anywhere. But my colleague explained that in their culture it would be inappropriate to proceed without this ritual. So I told him that he was definitely the one in charge of the dance.

There are simply too many variations in cultural strengths, strategies, and rituals to describe, even if we took an entire book just for that topic. But it is these strengths in individual communities that help ensure that CBPFA does not simply become a monolithic way of trying to force everyone to be the same. There is an expression that is understood in cultures around the world, "When you have a hammer, everything looks like a nail." When you have only one tool for providing psychological support, you are likely to use that one tool everywhere. One of the things that held back the development of psychological support around the world was that outside specialists would come to countries or cultures and try to impose their way of providing psychological support on the residents of those communities. In many cases, people rejected the psychological support because at least some aspects of the techniques were inappropriate in that community.

The advantage of CBPFA is that the psychological support package is adapted in each community to be appropriate for that community, and to incorporate the strengths of that culture into the CBPFA procedure. In this way, CBPFA avoids becoming the "hammer," and instead the process honors the local strengths and worldview. Having good mental health professionals involved in that process of adaptation will ensure that the scientifically supported aspects of the CBPFA are retained even while local traditions and perspectives are honored.

SUBJECT INDEX

Printed in Australia by Griffin Press
an Accredited ISO AS/NZS 14001:2004
Environmental Management System printer.